George Matheson

The Psalmist and the Scientist

Or, Modern Value of the Religious Sentiment

George Matheson

The Psalmist and the Scientist
Or, Modern Value of the Religious Sentiment

ISBN/EAN: 9783337008345

Printed in Europe, USA, Canada, Australia, Japan

Cover: Foto ©Lupo / pixelio.de

More available books at **www.hansebooks.com**

THE
PSALMIST AND THE SCIENTIST

OR

MODERN VALUE OF THE RELIGIOUS
SENTIMENT

BY

GEORGE MATHESON, M.A., D.D.

AUTHOR OF
'CAN THE OLD FAITH LIVE WITH THE NEW?' 'SPIRITUAL DEVELOPMENT
OF ST PAUL,' 'THE DISTINCTIVE MESSAGES OF THE OLD
RELIGIONS,' 'SACRED SONGS,' ETC.

THIRD EDITION

NEW YORK
DODD, MEAD, AND CO.
EDINBURGH AND LONDON
WILLIAM BLACKWOOD AND SONS
MDCCCXCIV

All Rights reserved

PREFACE.

I HAVE so fully indicated my purpose in the body of this work that a preface is almost superfluous. I design to inquire whether the religious sentiment of the past has been superannuated or rendered obsolete by the modern conception of nature. I have expressed respectively these seemingly opposite standpoints by the title, 'The Psalmist and the Scientist.' Science is confessedly the author of the modern conception of nature; the Book of Psalms is admittedly the repository of the religious sentiment in its largest and most comprehensive form. Of course it will be understood that the Psalms are here used not as an authority but as a type; the hymns of the Rig Veda would have served my purpose equally well if they had expressed the religious sentiment with equal catholicity. My present aim does not transcend the province of what is called natural religion. It is in some respects akin to that of Professor Seeley, but the thought moves on totally different lines and aspires to a less negative result. I have given few references, because, although this book has demanded much previous reading, its positions are neither to be affirmed nor denied on the authority of names. If it shall succeed in suggesting to abler and acuter minds any road of inquiry which may have been overlooked in the heat of discussion, if it shall stimulate some future explorer in the field of apologetics to examine more closely the relations of religion and science, the object of these pages shall be amply attained.

GEORGE MATHESON.

St Bernard's, Edinburgh.

CONTENTS.

CHAP.		PAGE
I.	INTRODUCTION,	1
II.	THE PSALMIST'S DEFENCE OF THE RELIGIOUS SENTIMENT,	18
III.	THE PSALMIST'S ARGUMENT FOR GOD,	47
IV.	THE PSALMIST'S VIEW OF THE ORIGIN OF LIFE,	85
V.	THE PSALMIST'S VIEW OF HUMAN INSIGNIFICANCE,	120
VI.	THE PSALMIST'S TWOFOLD CREATION,	138
VII.	THE PSALMIST'S GROUND OF RELIGIOUS CONFIDENCE,	157
VIII.	THE PSALMIST'S OPTIMISM,	180
IX.	THE PSALMIST'S PRINCIPLE OF SURVIVAL,	202
X.	THE PSALMIST'S PRINCIPLE OF SURVIVAL—(continued),	228
XI.	THE PSALMIST'S VIEW OF SIN,	253
XII.	THE PSALMIST'S PRINCIPLE OF CONSERVATION,	290
XIII.	CONCLUSION,	314

THE PSALMIST AND THE SCIENTIST.

CHAPTER I.

INTRODUCTION.

The religious sentiment is the earliest and the latest fruit of the religious spirit; it begins before the birth of dogma, and it survives after dogma has passed away. Men feel before they have learned to see. As in the individual life the first impressions of the mind are those of simple pleasure and pain, so in the life of the religious spirit the earliest impressions of the recipient are those of feeling and sentiment. And just as in the individual life it is by pleasurable and painful feeling that we reach our first knowledge of an outer world, so in the religious life it is by pleasurable and painful feeling that we reach our first perception of a world which transcends the outer. In neither case is the sentiment merely inward or subjective; in both it is an organ through which the human soul beholds something other than itself. The religious sentiment, like the element of sensuous feeling, is the earliest of those messengers which convey to us the tidings of a Power not ourselves. It begins before logic, before reasoning, before argument. It precedes all the forms of religious thought; it is antecedent to all the systems of theological speculation. And as it is earlier than the forms of dogmatic thought, so it is capable of surviving them. Our little systems may have their day and cease to be; but when they cease to be, it is only in order that they may give place to the systems of another day. What is the source of this reproduction? Why is it that when old theological formulas are quite extinguished there immediately appear in their room new expressions of dogmatic thought? There can be only one reason for this; there must be something which survives when the old form has perished, and which constitutes the link of connection between the old form and the new. That something we call the religious sentiment. It is that sense of divine truth which existed in the mind before it had obtained an explanation, and before it had received a name, and which, because it was independent of dogma in its origin, has been incapable of being destroyed by the dissolution of dogma; it survives to be the nucleus for the reconstruction of the system yet to be.

Now, what is the nature of this religious sentiment? The popular notion is that it is simply that minimum of religious belief which remains when all its essential articles have been destroyed, the last plank to which the drowning mariner may cling when the rest of the ship has gone to pieces. We are, for our part, quite convinced that this view is founded upon a delusion; it assumes that dogma is the staple of religious belief, and that sentiment belongs to a more limited sphere than dogma. We hold, on the other hand, that the sphere of religious sentiment is not distinct from the sphere of religious dogma—that the difference between them is not a difference of road, but a difference of vehicle. They both travel over the same way; the contrast between them lies in their mode of travelling. Dogma goes on foot; sentiment goes on the wing. The movement of the one is slow, measured, calculated; the movement of the other is a flight wherein the different points of the journey are almost instantaneously forgotten in the consummated goal. We have already pointed out that religious feeling is not simply a subjective or inward state—that equally with religious dogma it implies the presence of an object. We have now to add that the object of religious feeling may be identical with the object of religious dogma; what distinguishes the one from the other is not the thing perceived, but the mode of perceiving it. We may illustrate our meaning by a comparison drawn from the external senses. There are two modes in which I may learn the form of the same outward object—the touch and the sight. Let the object be one of considerable size placed within the reach of the hand; it will be possible for me by means of the hand to arrive at a perception of its form. But this perception will be reached not as a first but as a last result. My sense of the object's form will be attained not as an intuition, but as an inference. The whole will only be perceived when I have touched in detail the different parts, and when I have pieced these parts together by an act of imagination. But let me apply to the same object the sense of sight, and the result will be very different. In this case the perception of the form will be an immediate intuition, the first thing to be perceived. The whole will be seen before the parts; the vision of the object in itself will precede the examination of any of its constituent elements. Here, within the sphere of material nature, and in the region of natural sense, we have the illustration of a process by which the same object may at one and the same moment be looked upon in two totally different ways. It may be acted upon by two perceptions, each of which shall present it in a separate, in some respects in a contrary light. In the one case it may be viewed as a product of the reason, as something at whose form we arrive by an examination of its individual parts;

in the other, it may be presented as an immediate intuition of the mind, whose component elements must be studied in the light which itself has given.

Now, in the sphere of religion we are continually called to observe precisely the same process. Every doctrine may be metaphorically said to be an object either of touch or of sight. The man of the third century endeavoured to reach a knowledge of the person of Christ by manipulating one by one the different parts of His nature. He put his hand upon one side and declared it to be human; he touched the other and said it was divine. The result of the whole process was a composite Christ —a Christ in whose nature were amalgamated, without being blended, the ideas of divinity and humanity; some actions were assigned to the God, others were made peculiar to the Man. But the man of the first century looked upon the matter in a very different light. What he saw first of all was the whole Christ, the completed Christ, the Christ in His entire personality. He found in the person of Jesus something which appealed to his experience, and therefore he declared His person to be human; but he found in it at one and the same moment something which transcended his experience, and therefore he declared it to be divine. The divine and the human were not separate fields dividing the person of Jesus; the whole Son of Man was also the whole Son of God.

We have employed this illustration from the actual course of Church history, in order to make clear our view of the relation between religious dogma and religious sentiment. If our view be the true one, we shall be forced to modify some conclusions which we have formed in the past. Foremost among these is our belief that the shaking of religious dogma is equivalent to the shattering of religious conviction. Nothing is more common in our day than to hear men descant on the ravages which science has made on the dogmatic forms of the past. We are told that one by one the strongholds of former belief have been taken, and that the only remaining refuge for the spirit of man is to fall back from religious dogma into the sphere of religious life. Now there are worse places in which to reside than the sphere of religious life; the man who can live there has reached a permanent dwelling-place. But what we want to point out is, that in passing from dogma into life there is an intermediate region which the spirit of man may traverse. In leaving the sphere of dogma, he does not need to leave behind him the articles of his former faith. Intermediate between the intellectual form and the outward practice, there is a region conterminous with both, and uniting all that is best in each; it is that which we call the sphere of religious sentiment. The wine is not necessarily destroyed when the bottles are broken;

it may flow into a new receptacle. Religious belief is not necessarily shaken when those forms are shaken which originally contained it. The forms may be proved to be inadequate; they may be seen to be waxing old and ready to vanish away. It was thus that they appeared to him who wrote the Epistle to the Hebrews; he lived in a time of such transition that it seemed as if God were shaking not only the earth but the heavens. Yet it is to the author of this epistle that we are indebted for the thought that this shaking itself was only preparatory to a higher permanence. He declares that its real design was to show that there were things independent of dogma, which dogma could neither give nor take away. The earth and the heavens might be shaken, but it was only to manifest the fact that these were not the necessary supports of the religious life of man—that there were things which could not be shattered even by the passing away of the old heaven and the old earth. Behind the forms of religion there dwelt its spirit, its essence, its voice. God had in times past, in various modes and diverse parts, spoken to the fathers; the various modes and the diverse parts were being rapidly superseded by something new, but in the voice of the everlasting Father there was no variableness nor the least shadow of turning.

There is, then, a clear distinction between religious dogma and religious sentiment—a distinction not extending, indeed, to the truth perceived, but vividly affecting the mode of its perception. It is here, if anywhere, that we reach the explanation of a phenomenon in actual life which otherwise is incomprehensible; we allude to the apparent inconsistencies in the religious beliefs of great thinkers. Take, for example, such a man as Schleiermacher. When we look at him we seem to be in contact with two lives, and the two lives appear to be pulling in contrary directions. On one side we see the cold, calculating, critical intellect, analysing everything into its elements, and seeming to reduce these elements to the veriest minimum; on the other, we feel the presence and the power of an intensely earnest and a sincerely pious soul. Schleiermacher the critic is a sceptic, a man who weighs evidence and rejects everything which does not conform to his evidential standard; Schleiermacher the pastor is a simple believer, a man of religious feeling, faith, and prayer. How are we to reconcile these discrepancies? Shall we say that the great German thinker had different opinions at different times of the day? or shall we say that the attitude of the sceptic represented his reality, and the attitude of the pastor his acting? Neither; the explanation lies in a different region altogether. The dualism is to be sought, not in the nature of Schleiermacher, but in the nature of religious truth itself. There is a sphere of dogma and there is a sphere of sentiment, and what a man perceives in the sphere of dogma may not correspond in clearness to what he perceives in the sphere of sentiment. In the sphere of dogma he knows only in part, and the part which he knows is but an insignificant fragment of the whole; in the sphere of sentiment he sees the whole already completed, already fully realised. This is really what Paul means when he says, "We know in part, and we prophesy in part. But when that which is perfect is come, then that which is in part shall be done away." By "that which is perfect" he means, of course, love—the element of feeling as distinguished from the element of knowing. He means to imply that we can only know a doctrine by analysing its different parts, but that we can feel a doctrine without any analysis, in a moment, in the twinkling of an eye. This is the true explanation of Schleiermacher and of such men as Schleiermacher. It brings before us the fact that every religion consists of two sides, the articles and the prayer-book, and that the range of the prayer-book is in every case infinitely wider than the range of the articles. The schoolmen said that a thing might be philosophically false and yet theologically true. In this we cannot agree with them; but we can accept a somewhat analogous statement, that a thing may seem dogmatically false and yet be sentimentally true. The logical understanding deals only with the parts, and as it sees only a limited number of these, it is liable to behold contradictions; but the religious sentiment, beginning as it does with the perception of the whole, has from the outset a full and completed vision of that which the critical reason aspires to reach only at the end of all.

The Theism of the Old Testament, like every other religion, consists of two parts—the articles and the prayer-book. Its articles are implicitly contained in its cosmogony, in its history, and in its law. By combining the different elements of these we obtain a certain portraiture of the divine nature, which has stamped the Jewish religion with a mark of decided originality. This portraiture of the divine nature, constructed as it is out of the Jewish records of cosmogony, history, and law, has been vehemently assailed in each of its three component elements. It has been declared to be an inadequate expression of the God of creation, of the God of history, and of the God of moral government. In the present work we have no concern with these questions. We have simply to remark that the articles of every religion, whether inspired or uninspired, are bound to yield an inadequate expression of that which they seek to convey. Their expression is bound to be inadequate, for the simple reason that they *are* articles; in other words, dogmas or formulas of the understanding. It is impossible that the logical understanding can in a formula adequately represent any religious truth; there must always be something left unsaid, and this silent factor is itself a source of contradiction. But what we have to remark is this, that the articles of Old Testament Theism are only the half of its religion; it has another half—a prayer-book. Here, as elsewhere, the thoughts of the religious world have not been limited to dogmas or formulas; they have expressed themselves in emotions, in aspirations, in prayers. These emotions and aspirations have come down to us enshrined in a single volume which we call the Book of Psalms; it is distinctively the prayer-book of Old Testament theology. Little does the ordinary reader think that in perusing this prayer-book he is studying the religious life of centuries. It seems to him as if he were reading a work produced by a single mind in the course of a single year. And this is really the triumph and the vindication of the Old Testament prayer-book. We should naturally have expected to find that a work whose beginning is separated by so many centuries from its ending, would have revealed in its progress vast inequalities and extreme differences in the development of its individual parts. We should have thought that those portions of the book which had their rise in a primitive state of society would have been easily distinguishable from those which originated in the noonday of Jewish civilisation. It is not difficult to discover such a development in what we have called the dogmatic portion of Judaic Theism. The representation of God given in the

Book of Genesis is at once perceived to belong to a primitive age, and is seen to occupy the opposite remove in development from the representations given by the writers of Ecclesiastes and the Proverbs. But in the Psalms the modern reader looks in vain for any such evidence of mental evolution. It is not difficult, indeed, to assign certain dates to certain psalms—to say that one belongs to the age of David, another to the age of Solomon, and a third to the age of the Captivity; but this is done through the accident of historical reference or the peculiarities of linguistic construction. The conclusion is in no sense reached by a comparison of different thoughts which mark different epochs. Such a comparison is here out of the question, because the difference of thought does not exist. The earliest psalm breathes the same spirit as the latest, and breathes it with an equal intensity. We feel that we are here, not in a region of progress, not in a world of development; we are under the presence of one unchanging sky, and we never for an instant lose the sense of youth's morning. The spirit of the Jewish prayer-book is a spirit of perpetual youth; and when everything else in the nation reveals the signs of waxing old, the fervent devotion of its psalms preserves the glow of its spring-time.

Now this is as it should be. Genuine sentiment never grows old to the heart, never becomes an anachronism to the life of the spirit. We are constantly reminded of this in the study of ancient history. Often when we are perusing the annals of an age whose civilisation and institutions lie far behind our own, we are arrested by some trait of feeling which in a moment dispels the anachronism and recalls us to the eternal brotherhood of man. There is perhaps no period more completely divorced from our intellectual sympathies than the days of the Israelitish judges. It has been called the Iron Age. It is separated from our life, from our manners, from our civilisation, by the length and breadth of a whole universe; and one feels, in studying its annals, that he is in the presence of something with which his mind has no contact. But even as this thought passes through him, he is arrested in the very heart of this age by a spectacle which reminds him of the eternity of human nature. It is in this barbarous sphere of the Israelitish judges that we are confronted by that touching story of sacrificial love which is enshrined in the Book of Ruth. The picture of filial devotion is as modern as any incident of the present day; and it is as a picture of the present day that we reverence and prize it: we feel that it expresses a sentiment which is independent of human development. Now this is precisely the feeling with which the great prayer-book of the Jewish nation is regarded by every devout mind. It is an oasis in a desert of time.

It comes to us from the depth of a past whose annals lie behind us, whose opinions we have surmounted, whose institutions we have far outgrown. Yet we are compelled to confess that *it* is not outgrown. The prayers which it breathes, the aspirations which it utters, are as fresh to-day as they were in the days of Solomon. They have been altogether unaffected by the lapse of time or the changes of life. And here is the proof: we never associate them with any time. We do not say that they are David's, or that they are Solomon's; we accept them as our own. We appropriate them as the direct and exact expression of the need which now presses upon our hearts, and we value them precisely for the fact that they do express our needs. It is the utter absence of any sense of anachronism in these prayers — the utter freedom from any reference to a stage of surmounted development— that constitutes them the prayer-book of the Gentile as much as of the Jew: they belong to the things of the heart, and therefore they are unchangeable and eternal.

Thus much, indeed, every one will admit. It will not be denied by any that the Psalms do not present any sense of anachronism to the heart. But a more important question remains. Do they present that sense of anachronism to the intellect? Admitting that the feelings which they awaken have lost nothing of their freshness, does it follow that these feelings still represent realities? The poetry of the psalmist retains to our poetic faculty the same beauty which it had to him, but we know that to him it was something more than poetry; it was fact: is it still fact to us? Modern science has assailed and shaken many ancient fortresses; have the sentiments of this prayer-book been amongst the things that cannot be shaken? Science has attacked the articles one by one. It has attacked the ancient conception of God, and has refused any longer to accept the notion of an architect living outside of the machine. It has attacked the old idea of creation, and has refused any longer to believe that the world, as we know it, could have emerged into being in a moment and in the twinkling of an eye. It has attacked the conception of miracle which was held by the men of old time, and has denied that the world as it now exists can manifest any violation of law. It has attacked the primitive notions of moral government, and has rejected that view of divine action which has been content to see God only in the superintendence of a single people. All this science has done, and is still doing. What effect it has produced, it is not our province here to say. In the opinion of many, it has rendered it henceforth impossible that the articles of ancient Theism can ever again be restated in their original form. Assuming that it be so, we have still to remind the reader that the articles are only the one half of the religion, and we have still to ask the scientist what is his relation to the other half. If it be conceded that we can no longer through the medium of the understanding look at the old truths in the old way, can we look at them in the old way through the medium of the heart? We do not merely ask if the sentiments of the Jewish prayer-book can still be cherished by the poetic faculty. Lange, in his 'History of Materialism,' has laboured to show that although religion be expelled as an outward reality, it may and ought still to be preserved as a product of art and imagination. We cannot admit that either art or imagination could survive for a single year, unless they were believed to represent some great reality; we cannot allow that the visions of the poet would for a moment charm, if there were not in the mind of the beholder a deep-seated hope that somewhere and at some time they might prove to be true. And if it be so even with the professed products of imagination, it must be emphatically so with the spirit of religion. No man's religious devotion could subsist for an hour if he believed it to be the expression of a mere subjective feeling, if he refused to recognise the hope that it might have a corresponding reality. The question, therefore, which we have to ask of science is this, Is the religious sentiment of the psalmist an anachronism? Has any discovery been made in the realm of physical nature which has reduced that sentiment to the rank of a mere poetic dream? Has the change in our conception of the universe which the nineteenth century has confessedly seen, involved a mitigation or an annihilation of the value of that spirit of devotion which influenced and dominated the minds of the men of old time? That is the question which these pages seek to answer.

Meantime we have to remark that the prayer-book of the Jewish nation itself seeks to furnish a reason for the hope which is in it. The religious sentiment of the Book of Psalms is very far from being a religious sentimentalism; it contains an argument for its own existence. There is an argument in feeling as well as in reasoning; they differ only in their method. The argument of reason mounts on steps to its goal; the argument of feeling flies on wings. The former can vindicate its every stage, the latter can only vindicate its completed ascent; but the effect in each case is the same. There are sentiments which produce conviction as powerfully as the most elaborate demonstration, and to the sense of whose certainty the most elaborate demonstration could not add. The Book of Psalms enfolds within itself a reason for its own being. What is that reason? What is that process of argument by which the prayer-book of the Jewish nation vindicates its own existence and maintains its right to be? The answer to that question shall be the subject of our next chapter.

CHAPTER II.

THE PSALMIST'S DEFENCE OF THE RELIGIOUS SENTIMENT.

Psalm cxlv. 15, 16; xlii. 1, 2; lxxxiv. 1-3.

We have placed these three passages in this order, because when taken in this order they reveal a connected argument—an argument, it is true, whose basis is not reason but feeling, but which is none the less secure on that account. The first step of the process will be found in Ps. cxlv. 15, 16: "The eyes of all wait upon Thee; and Thou givest them their meat in due season. Thou openest Thine hand, and satisfiest the desire of every living thing." The psalmist is not arguing, not moralising, not laying down a thesis; he is praying. He is engaged in that which is the preliminary part of all prayer—thanksgiving. His words are meant to express, not the dictum of a logician, but the burst of gratitude which flows from a devout soul. None the less the burst of gratitude is expressive of a great thought.

He declares that in the world of animated nature all things are double, that there is everywhere a correspondence between the organism and its environment. Within the living organism there exist certain definite desires, and each of these has been met by an object which satisfies it. The world of living nature, as it appears to the eye of the psalmist, reveals a world without and a world within; and between this world without and this world within there subsists the strictest harmony. He has no theory about this harmony; he does not say, with Leibnitz, that it is a pre-established harmony—or, with the modern doctrine of evolution, that it is a harmony resulting from the adjustment of the organism to its environment: these theories belong to the domain of reason, and the psalmist is a man of feeling. He therefore contents himself with saying that the adaptations in the physical world are the law of God: "Thou openest Thine hand, and satisfiest the desire of every living thing."

Will the scientist admit them to be the law of *nature?* If so, he has conceded that the sentiment of the psalmist is no anachronism. When the scientist speaks of nature, he always sees the word in his mind's eye printed with a capital letter. Even to the most materialistic of the class, nature is something more than that which we see, hear, and touch; it is at the very least the manifestation of a great inscrutable Force. We shall therefore not here dispute about the use of a term; our sole concern is with the fact. The question is, whether the sentiment of the Israelitish psalmist be or be not an anachronism in the view of modern science, whether it be or be not one of the things which cannot be shaken? And to this question science itself returns a decided answer. The most modern definition of life which has been stamped with the *imprimatur* of science is one which is actually based on a recognition of that truth which the psalmist saw. Life is in our days said to consist in the adaptation of the organism to its environment. When the psalmist declared that every living thing derived its satisfaction from an outward accommodation to its desires, he arrived in other words at the same conclusion. He saw around him in the life of every organism certain appetites, wants, needs. He beheld hungering and thirsting, an eye waiting for the light and an ear waiting for the breath of sound. It occurred to him to ask, What if these wants had found no supply in nature? What if nature had implanted a hunger without food, a thirst without drink, an eye without light, an ear without the breath of sound? It was in putting this question to himself that the psalmist awoke to a sense of the real benevolence of nature. He saw that this benevolence consisted just in giving to each organism its environment, just in supplying that object which its want specially required. He felt that the Author of the universe had shown His love for the universe in instituting a law of correspondence, whereby every living creature found outside of itself the complement of that which lay within it; and he expressed his adoration of that love in the voice of thanksgiving: "The eyes of all wait upon Thee; and Thou givest them their meat in due season."

We are now prepared to take the second step. We shall find it in the transition from Ps. cxlv. 15, 16, to Ps. xlii. 1, 2. We have seen that in the view of the psalmist every natural desire has a right to its object. He now goes on to declare that the desire for God is as natural as any other necessity of life: "As the hart panteth after the water-brooks, so panteth my soul after Thee, O God. My soul thirsteth for God, for the living God: when shall I come and appear before God?" The idea is that the thirst of the soul for God has as much its seat in nature as the thirst of the hart for the water-brooks. That religion is natural to man is admitted by all science. Men whose systems diverge from one another in many respects, and whose creeds diverge in all respects from orthodoxy, have been unanimous in recognising that the religious life of man is a positive factor of human nature which needs to be accounted for. Auguste Comte, after relegating theology to the limbo of the past, concludes his scientific career by instituting a religion of humanity. G. H. Lewes, one of the best types of positivism which England has produced, has, in his 'Problems of Life and Mind,' no scruple in recording his conviction that in the age of the future, religion will not die. Lange, as we have already seen, although himself practically a materialist, advocates in the interest of poetry the cultivation of the religious faculty. Dr Carpenter, in his 'Mental Physiology,' does not hesitate to express his belief in the universality of that sentiment which has prompted man to seek for God. Herbert Spencer, himself the apostle of modern evolution, has devoted the opening chapters of his work on 'First Principles' to show that the ultimate object of religion is the ultimate object of science. These converging testimonies from minds in other respects so widely varying, may be taken as affording conclusive evidence that the opinion of the modern scientist is on this head not opposed to the sentiment of the ancient psalmist, and that in our days, as in his own, the religious thirst of the human soul is admitted to be as natural as the hart's thirst for the water-brooks.

We pass, therefore, to the third of those steps taken by the mind of the psalmist. It will be found in Ps. lxxxiv. 1-3: "How amiable are Thy tabernacles, O Lord of hosts! My soul longeth, yea, even fainteth for the courts of the Lord: my heart and my flesh crieth out for the living God. Yea, the sparrow hath found an house, and the swallow a nest for herself, where she may lay her young, even thine altars, O Lord of hosts, my King, and my God." Let us understand what is the meaning of these words. The psalmist virtually says: If the thirst for God be as natural to man as any other appetite of human nature, and if every appetite of human nature has found its satisfaction in correspondence with an outward object, shall the thirst for God be the only thing in the nature of man which has nothing to correspond to it either in the heavens above or in the earth beneath? Shall the religious instinct of the human soul be the one unsatisfied instinct, the one hunger of man for which there has been provided no food, the one thirst for which there has been supplied no water? There is a tabernacle for everything in nature, a house in which every desire can find shelter and sustenance. The sparrow hath found a house, and the swallow a nest for herself; the hart has discovered the water-brooks for which she panted. My soul is of more value than many sparrows, yet my soul longeth, fainteth; it cries out for tabernacles which it has not yet found amongst the things which are seen and temporal; it stands in the open air and waits for a dwelling-place. Surely there cannot exist such an anomaly in nature; surely there must be somewhere in the universe a resting-place for the spirit of man, corresponding to those resting-places which nature has provided for the natural lives of all.

This is really the sentiment of the psalmist, and it is a sentiment in which there is deep philosophy. He is impressed beyond measure with the comparative unrest of man in creation. He is struck with the fact that the correspondence between the desire and its object prevails so universally in the lower spheres, and seems to disappear in the highest of all. He marvels that there should be provided a house for the sparrow and a nest for the swallow, and yet that the spirit of man should seem betimes to be wandering through dry places seeking rest and finding none. He is convinced that such a state of things cannot be permanent, must of necessity be transient and evanescent. He is satisfied that there is somewhere an environment for the spiritual nature of the human soul, a divine tabernacle within which its restless longings may repose, and by whose shelter its religious life may be explained and vindicated. Without such an explanation and vindication, the religious life of man is to him the anomaly of anomalies.

The sentiment expressed in this psalm is by no means an isolated one in the Jewish prayer-book, otherwise we might have been content to assign it a merely historical reference. We might have refused to see in it anything beyond the fact that an exile from his native land yearned to behold the ancient courts of worship, and envied even the swallows that still built their nests there. That this was the historical origin of the words we have not the slightest doubt; but had they rested in their origin, they never would have become part of the national prayer-book. What gave them their place in that book was the fact that the circumstance which first suggested them was merely a metaphor expressive of a great principle. It expressed a principle, moreover, which had already found a place in the sacred songs of Israel. We find, as it seems to us, a forecast of the same sentiment in the language of Ps. xxxvi. 5-7. The psalmist is there speaking of the universal adaptations of the benevolence of God throughout the visible universe. What he designs to say is this: The divine mercy stretches over all the works of creation. The Lord preserveth "man and beast," *i.e.*, natural life in all its phases, human and animal. If He preserves man generically, shall He not preserve man spiritually? Shall not the *children* of men—those who have in them the ripeness and the fulness of human nature—"put their trust under the shadow of His wings"? If there are pleasures adapted to the thirst of the physical creation, surely these latest products of the creative spirit shall be made to drink of the river of the pleasures of God.

We see the same thought in a somewhat modified form in the concluding verses of Ps. xvii., although the psalmist is there contrasting, not man with the rest of creation, but the spiritual man with those who are unspiritual. He tells us that unspiritual men have in the present life an abundant fulness; every faculty is satisfied because each faculty is adapted to its environment. But then, in striking contrast to this, he concludes with the words: "As for me, I will behold Thy face in righteousness: I shall be satisfied, when I awake, with Thy likeness." He feels that his spiritual nature cannot claim in the meantime any such adaptation to its environment. He feels that in fact his spiritual nature is mainly distinguished just by the absence of such adaptation, just by the sense of vacancy which it experiences when it tries to rest in tabernacles of clay. None the less is he persuaded that in the universe as a whole there can exist no such anomaly. He knows that somewhere there must be found for the spirit of man that which will bring it into harmony with all other faculties and desires, and he expresses this conviction in words which already breathe the hope of immortality: "I shall be satisfied, when I awake, with Thy likeness."

We have now to ask, Is this an anachronism? Is it capable of standing unshaken in the light of modern science? Is there any way in which the conclusion may be evaded that the spiritual nature of man ought to have that adaptation to its needs which all temporal natures reveal? There are two ways in which it may be attempted to evade this conclusion, and as they frequently present themselves to our view in the discussion of this subject, we shall take leave briefly to estimate their leadings.

In the first place, it has been said that the religious sentiment is not a distinct or separate power of the human mind. We are asked what right we have to assume that the tendency of man towards an object of religious worship is an original and underived part of his nature. We are told, on the contrary, that so far from being a simple and independent faculty, the instinct of worship is a sentiment made up of several feelings, and only acquires unity in their blending. We are told that the religious sentiment is a combination of at least three other sentiments—the impression of fear, the sense of dependence, and the feeling of wonder. Man at first trembled before the majesty of visible nature, then submitted himself resignedly to that majesty, and ultimately, as the sense of freedom woke within him, began to wonder and admire. The instinct of worship comes from the blending of these different shades, and therefore it has no right to claim that special environment which should only belong to a special power.

Now it is not our intention to dispute here the truth of this doctrine. Were we disposed to be metaphysical, we might perhaps pertinently ask how the religious sentiment can be a union of two such contrary elements as the sense of abject dependence and the sense of childlike wonder; the one is a stage of necessity, the other is a realisation of freedom. It is very easy, indeed, to see how a sense of abject dependence can be *followed* by a feeling of childlike wonder; this is in accordance with historical fact, and in harmony with the law of human development. But it is a very different thing to say that these two elements can coalesce, and that in their coalition they can produce something which has all the appearance of a spiritual unity. As we have said, however, we have no wish to dispute the point, for it is not on this ground that we would defend the scientific value of the psalmist's argument. If we refuse to be swayed by the objection before us, it is on a totally different ground, and one which cannot be shaken by any speculative reasoning. Suppose we concede that the religious sentiment is not originally a simple and independent faculty, but has been built up by the combination of other feelings. What then? Would it follow from this that the religious sentiment has no right to claim an environment, no right to assume that there is somewhere an object adapted to it? Assuredly not. For, what are the facts of the case? Those powers and faculties of the human mind which *have* received an environment and an adaptation are, according to modern science, not one of them in their origin simple and independent. Nothing appears more original and underived than the sense of sight; and yet it is the doctrine of modern science that the sense of sight, like all the other organs of sensation, is only the last result of a neural process, a perception whose unity has been constituted by the coalition and the blending of a variety of nervous impressions. Such, in the view of modern science, is the origin of those natural faculties by which we commune with the external world. But the point to be observed is this, that in spite of their composite origin these faculties *do* commune with the external world. Although in their origin they are not special powers, they become special powers in their combination; and the moment they become special powers, they receive a special environment. Whatever the human eye was in its initial stage, it is assuredly a human eye now, a power which in its final completeness is altogether unlike any other power. And just on account of this ultimate unlikeness to other things, the human eye has now received an environment specially adapted to its nature, and quite unadapted to any other nature. The controversy whether light was made for the eye or the eye made for light is idle here; we keep to the scientific admission that the one is adapted to the other, that the one is the environment of the other. Keeping to that admission and accepting the scientific account of the eye's composite origin, we arrive at the definite conclusion that, wherever a natural faculty becomes special, whatever its origin may have been, it immediately receives in the outer world an avenue of communion suited to its nature. Now the psalmist asks no more for that faculty which we call supernatural, but which really claims to be an integral part of human nature. It is in virtue of its claim to naturalness, it is in virtue of its right to be considered a normal phase of our humanity, that the religious sentiment demands an object corresponding to its nature. It asks by what authority or by what law it is put out of uniformity with existing things; why, alone of all organs, alone of all faculties, alone of all desires, it should be left without a dwelling-place, without an environment, without an object with which it may commune. It asks, in the interest of science, in the interest of that regularity of law which science delights to preach, why the law of adaptation should in one solitary instance be violated, and violated precisely in that instance in which the power that seeks environment has greatest pretensions to originality. Its language is still substantially the language of the psalmist when he inquires why his spiritual nature should faint and long when the sparrow hath an house and the swallow a nest.

But this brings us to consider a second objection which may be made to the conclusiveness of the psalmist's reasoning—an objection which is commonly used against the argument from design, but which, if sustained, must bear with equal force against the principle of adaptation in general. We allude to the doctrine frequently promulgated that there are useless organs in the world. It is alleged that both in the framework of the animal creation and in the constitution of the human body there are discoverable certain organs for which no use can be found, and whose absence in some cases would be a positive advantage. If this fact be conceded, it will be pertinently asked, By what law of reasoning does the prayer-book of the Jewish nation claim an object for the religious faculty? Why should not this religious faculty be itself just one of those elements of human nature which are works of supererogation—just one of those things for which no purpose can be found in the earth, or in the heavens, and which, because they have nothing adapted to them, can only be sources of pain? Why should not the unrest of the religious sentiment, the disquietude which it awakens in the heart of man, be simply an evidence of its superfluity in the scheme of creation, and a proof that its absence would be the evolution of a higher good?

Now here, as in the former objection, we do not intend to dispute the truth of the alleged fact that there are certain individual forms in which organs have been discovered without a purpose. We are far indeed from admitting the fact. Volumes of theology have been written in disproof of it, but none of these have impressed us so powerfully as the candid concession of one whose interest lay in establishing the negation of purpose. The argument which seems to us conclusive against the existence of useless organs in nature, is that of evolution itself as advocated by Professor Huxley.[1] Professor Huxley advances in the interest of evolution a strong argument against the perpetuation of faculties which have no work to do. He tells us, and tells us truly, that according to the laws of evolution, a faculty or organ can only be kept in life by being kept in exercise. He tells us that if a faculty or organ should by any chance pass into a state of quiescence —in other words, should cease to be of any use—it will in process of time inevitably cease to live. In the Mammoth cave of Kentucky there is dense darkness. It is inhabited by fishes which are not only without sight, but have merely rudimentary eyes. Are we to suppose that the fishes were created without perfect organs because it was foreseen that they should live in darkness? Such a supposition is no longer tenable. But another supposition remains; it is, that by reason of long disuse the organ itself has become imperfect and is gradually disappearing. This is precisely what, according to Professor Huxley, would follow from the lengthened disuse of any organ.

[1] See his article in criticism of Haeckel, in the collected volume of his essays published in 1871.

Weighty, however, as this reasoning seems, and all the more weighty because it is the concession of one not favourable to teleology, we do not intend on this occasion to avail ourselves of its candour. We shall take for granted, for the sake of the argument, the averment that there are useless organs in nature — that is to say, that there exist at the present time certain individual forms which reveal the presence of organs that have no present purpose. It is very important that the doctrine should be expressed in this roundabout and qualified way, because, if expressed absolutely, it would not be the doctrine of modern science. No votary of modern science, whether Christian, theist, or atheist, ever held or ever asserted that the so-called useless organs of nature were useless organs from the beginning. What the adherents of this doctrine hold is simply this: There is in the body of a certain animal a part of the structure which is at present useless, if not even hurtful. But this animal was itself originally derived from the life of another animal, and that again from a still earlier structure. The organ in the latest product is useless simply because its day is past. It is the survival of an earlier culture. In the ancestors of this recent animal the organ had its function, like all other things; it was exactly adapted to the environment of that primitive age. But the old environment is gone; the waves have receded and left it high and dry on the beach. It exists as the monument of a past, as the relic of a time when things were different from what they now are, and its uselessness in the present generation proceeds from the fact that it has exhausted all its strength in the effort to serve its own day.

Admitting then that there are such organs, is the religious sentiment one of them? If we answer in the affirmative, let us observe what follows. Nothing less than the destruction of that theory of evolution which is now scientifically accepted as the law of natural development. Those powers which by supposition are superseded in their function, are by supposition powers which have been outgrown by the race which has lost the use of them. But the claim of the religious sentiment is nothing less than the claim to be in communion with a divine nature. Will it then be said that the communion with a divine nature which is now denied to man, was possessed originally by the beast of the field, the fowl of the air, and the fish of the sea? Will it be said that the environment of the religious life which is refused to a rational soul, was possessed at the beginning by creatures devoid of that attribute to which we give the name of reason? The pessimist Hartmann has advanced a view somewhat analogous to this: he says that in the passage from the animal to the man there has been lost a sense; humanity is poorer by one faculty than the beast of the field. But then Hartmann, in advancing this theory, is quite prepared to take the inevitable inference, and does take it—the inference, namely, that Darwinism is a delusion and modern science an error. He rejects the modern doctrine of scientific development, on the ground that the development is not upwards but downwards, and that in passing from the animal to the human we have passed from the higher to the lower. We may safely say that in the light of such a conclusion the modern scientist will prefer to revert to the view of the psalmist.

There is, then, no scientific anachronism in that sentiment of the Jewish prayer-book which causes the heart of man to claim an environment for his religious faculty, which leads him to seek for the instinct of his worship an object in the outward world such as all other instincts possess. But now, driven by the exigencies of the argument, there are some who have placed the difficulty on another field. Granted, they say, that the religious life of man, like all other phases of his life, must have an object adapted to it in the outer universe. Why should that object be sought where other objects are not sought?—in the supernatural. Why should not nature itself be the object of the religious faculty, or of that power called by whatever name whereby man desires to commune with something beyond him? Doubtless the religious sentiment, like every other impulse of our being, must have its environment in some object of the surrounding world; but why should not that object be the surrounding world itself? Is it not a monstrous leap in the reasoning process to bound to the conclusion that because every sense has its adaptation in natural things, the religious sense must have its adaptation in supernatural things? Would we not expect the inference to be exactly the reverse of this?

Now we freely admit that if the object of the religious sentiment be conceived as supernatural in its adaptation, we have reached a conclusion out of harmony with all nature; a supernatural adaptation to natural faculties is a contradiction in terms. The very notion of adaptation is the notion of correspondence—that is to say, of a certain uniformity of character between the object communed with and the power with which it communes. However transcendent be the object of our religious worship, it can only be an object of true worship in so far as it is understood by us—in other words, in so far as it is in contact with our own life. If any man likes to call the object of his religious worship by the name Nature, we shall make no objection. We cannot object to any name which expresses the fact that the Being whom we worship is worshipped by us by reason of a congruity between His life and ours. All worship must be founded on communion, and that with which a man communes must ever be natural to him. If, therefore, any one shall choose to give to the Being with whom he communes the name of Nature, we shall refuse to see anything irreverent in the act. We shall only insist that he who gives to his deity this name, shall use the word in no partial or limited sense. We shall insist that in calling God Nature, he will mean something more than any particular object in nature, such as sun, or moon, or stars. We shall insist that he shall employ the term in its etymological and only rightful sense, to express all that *is*. He must use it to designate not a particular phase of being, either physical, intellectual, or moral, but that which comprehends even while it transcends them all, which binds their diversities into a common unity, and makes them one. Above all, he must be careful not to exclude from his conception of nature any element which now exists within it—not to leave out of account from his estimate of the universe any portion of that universe which is now a matter of experience. Accordingly, he will give scrupulous attention to incorporate in his idea of nature the idea of life. The manifestation of life is nature's latest product, but in a question of this kind time counts for nothing. However it came and whenever it came, it is now as much a part of nature as any mass of matter or any atom of space. As such, it must be accounted for—that is to say, it must be counted in the estimate. He who speaks of God as Nature, must understand a living Nature—a principle which, whatever else it may contain, contains assuredly the element of life.

Now it is worth while remarking that this seems to be the condition on which the Jewish prayer-book insists beyond all others—the association of the object of our worship with the idea of life. It is not very particular about the name it gives to the Deity; sometimes it says Elohim, sometimes Jehovah. But the one thing on which it insists is, that its God shall be a living God. That for which the soul of the psalmist thirsts is a fountain of life—an object which, by community of life, can commune with his own nature. "My soul thirsts for God, for the living God." One would almost imagine that he had in his mind certain prevalent conceptions of God, which made religion "a dry, parched land." There were some amongst the Jewish theologians who, in their excessive desire to emphasise the *personality* of God, had made Him less than a *living* God. They had driven Him back into the remotest circle of the universe, and had placed Him there on an inapproachable throne. They had made His personality so distinct from all other personalities, that His life was incommunicable to any other life. Men believed in His existence as they believed in the existence of a land beyond the sea, whose shores they had no means of ever reaching. And so it came to pass that the place of the living God was supplied by a hierarchy of angels. The chasm between earth and heaven was filled up in the imagination of the worshipper by a ladder of intermediate intelligences, on whose steps the humble suppliant might send up his petition to the throne of the Eternal. It was this conception of the universe which the soul of the psalmist repudiated. He thirsted for something more direct, more immediate, more divine. He was weary of having his prayers transmitted through second-hand agencies; he felt that such agencies were really further removed from him than was the Supreme Fountain of life. There had dawned within his heart the sense of a unity between himself and that Eternal whom he worshipped, the conviction that there was something in his own nature which responded to the nature of God. With such a conviction, he chafed at the thought that he was made to send his messages through ambassadors in whose image he was not made and to whose nature he was not allied. He felt that he would be nearer to his goal if he could break down the celestial ladder and rise on the wings of a dove into personal communion and rest. He wanted to see the life which he believed to throb at the heart of the universe break forth from its isolation in the heart and penetrate through the arteries, to feel its pulsations everywhere and always, alike in the rise of an empire and in the fall of a sparrow. The God whom he desired to worship was a God who should permeate the length and the breadth, the height and the depth of all being, and in whose universal presence all things should live and move.

Such was the thirst of the psalmist as expressed in the Jewish prayer-book; the question is, Is this thirst an anachronism? That men have still the same longing will be denied by none; but has the longing any longer an object to correspond with it? The psalmist in his day believed that there was a life in nature corresponding to the aspirations of his living soul, and the presence of such a belief was itself a source of strength. Have we in our days lost the right to believe? Has the advance of modern science compelled us to banish from our conception of physical nature that element of life which constituted to the mind of the Jew the only source of physical beauty? Are we no longer entitled to regard the natural universe as anything more than a piece of mechanism knit together by wires and propelled by unintelligent forces? If so, we must indeed cease to call God by the name of Nature, or to invest the idea of nature with any association of worship; it becomes an anachronism to print with a capital letter that which in our conception has ceased to be alive.

But on what evidence are we asked to give up this primitive hope? On what grounds are we required to believe that nature as a collective unity is devoid of the principle of intelligent life? It is surely fair, before coming to such a tremendous conclusion, to weigh carefully, calmly, and dispassionately the premisses on which it professes to be based. These premisses, indeed, are not difficult to find and very easy to state. We are told that the investigations of modern science are gradually tending to the conclusion that all things in the universe have originally come from one thing, and that this one thing was a mass of matter. All the varieties of creation, what we call material and what we call immaterial alike, suns and systems, trees and mountains, animals and men, were, we are told, originally comprehended within the folds of a fire-cloud. Whatever differences now prevail between them have been after-growths; at the beginning, all things were indistinguishable. Mind with its lofty pretensions can claim no higher origin than the flower of the field, and the flower of the field can claim no superior pedigree to the most insensate atom of matter.

Such is the doctrine of a large section of the scientific world. It stands at the farthest remove from our own personal belief. We believe, and shall in a subsequent chapter endeavour to show, that the original element out of which creation was evolved could not have been matter. But we are not yet ripe for this inquiry, and we do not wish to anticipate its conclusion. We shall, accordingly, sink on this occasion our own personal convictions, and shall endeavour for the sake of the argument to meet on its own ground the materialistic section of the scientific world. We shall assume in the meantime that the scientific materialist is right. We shall take it for granted that he has proved his case, that he has established beyond controversy the position that the original element of creation was an element of matter. The question is, If it be so, what then? What the scientific materialist wants to prove is, that the sentiment of the Jewish prayer-book is an anachronism, that the belief in a living intelligent Nature can no longer be held. The argument by which he professes to prove this, is the reduction of all things to a materialistic origin. Let us suppose that this position had been established, would the conclusion follow? It is almost universally taken for granted that the proof of materialism would henceforth render impossible our belief in an intelligent principle in nature. Standing as we do at the farthest pole from materialism, we are bound to confess that the inference has always seemed to us a premature one. Let us imagine that a revelation were made to the human race of its origination from dead matter, that it were clearly and demonstrably revealed to man that his whole mental constitution had been simply the product of what is called protoplasm—would it follow from this, that men would thenceforth be illogical in having an object of religious worship, or in recognising that object as a concrete intelligence? So far from being illogical, we hold that the reversion to such a worship would be strictly in accordance with the principles of materialistic reasoning. For, might not the worshipper argue thus: If dead matter has been able within a limited compass to produce such a wonderful intelligence as mine, why should it not with an infinite compass produce an infinite Intelligence? If within a narrow sphere protoplasm has been able to bring forth this wondrous thing which I call my life, is it not reasonable to suppose that in the unlimited spheres of nature it may have brought forth a life commensurate with the vastness of the universe? May not that life have been eternally begotten? The scientist tells me that matter had no beginning: may not its living superstructure have been also without beginning? And if I am allowed to go so far, may I not logically go further? If this life of mine, which is by supposition the product of protoplasm, has been able to dominate over that which made it, why should not the Infinite life, which is by supposition the product of material nature, be also able to dominate over that which is the basis of its being? If I, notwithstanding my material origin, have become a providence to things beneath me, may not the life of nature be a Providence to the course of nature? Nay, am I not entitled on these premises to take yet higher ground? If I with my life hypothetically derived from material principles am yet able to impart my being to future generations, why should not this Infinite life, whose origin is also supposed to be material, be able in like manner to impart itself to mankind? Is not the possibility of immortality itself involved in this analogy? If the life of nature be a life which exhibits no diminution in its forces, would not its impartation to me make me partaker of its indestructibility? Finally, if life as it exists in me is able to reveal itself to life as it exists in my brother man, why should not life as it exists in nature be able to reveal itself to my life? If criticism should prove, which it never has proved, that no such revelation has yet been given, how would that demonstrate that no such revelation ever will be given? Might it not be that the revelation itself had to wait for the development of the creature, and that the principle of scientific evolution might itself usher the life of creation into the glorious liberty of the sons of God?

You say this is, after all, but a poor conception of God. Undoubtedly it is—that is to say, it is poor when weighed against the riches of that thought of God which we derive from Christianity. But we must remember that religious worship existed long before the dawn of Christianity, and that in the large majority of cases the pre-Christian conception of God was no richer than this. Nay, it is not too much to say that in the large majority of cases the pre-Christian conception of God was to all intents and purposes exactly this conception. The God of heathendom was for the most part not a being who created the universe, but a being whom the universe created. The Brahma of Hindu worship had his origin in a neuter principle analogous to what we understand by dead matter. The incarnations of Buddha were the coming into life and into personality of a principle which originally was impersonal, and which had risen into the rank of deity through a succession of transmigrations. The Logos of Philo was conceived to be an intelligent spirit who had risen or been developed out of the inanimate universe; the origin from which he sprang was a parentage from something as dead as matter, and he ruled over a universe to which he owed his very being. Meagre and unsatisfactory as such conceptions were, they constituted for centuries the faith of millions of the human race. To such a God as this were poured forth the prayers of hundreds of thousands. The religious sentiment proved itself able to exist in a state of things analogous to that which would be produced by the establishment of scientific materialism. The inference is not unreasonable that the establishment of scientific materialism would be followed by a regress towards this surmounted standpoint — a regress miserable and deplorable indeed when compared with the light of Christianity, yet evidencing even in its decay the continuity and imperishableness of the religious sentiment.

But now, having for the sake of the argument taken the lowest room, are we bound to remain there? Whatever the sentiment of pagan antiquity may have been, the God of the Jewish prayer-book was a God who created all things, a Being who was not the product of material mechanism, but Himself the producer and the soul of the mechanism of nature. It remains, therefore, to ask on this branch of the subject, whether this higher conception of God is itself unscientific, whether the advance of modern research can ever shake this claim of the religious consciousness to place the object of its worship in the background and at the origin of all existing things. A consideration of the psalmist's position on this question will engage us in the following chapter.

CHAPTER III.

THE PSALMIST'S ARGUMENT FOR GOD.

Psalm xciv. 9-11.

In our last chapter we considered the psalmist's evidence for the existence of a religious sentiment; we have now to consider his view of the object of that sentiment. He has proved that there is ground for the belief in the existence of some higher Power adapted to the religious nature of man; he now proceeds to show what is the character of that Power. The point which he wishes to establish is, not the being but the personality of God. He takes it for granted that there *is* a Power which has planted the ear, formed the eye, and given understanding to the human soul; what he wants to know is whether the Power which can thus confer intelligence can itself be less than intelligent. Our first impression is that the argument is labour thrown away. Is it not a truism, we say, to seek to establish a point which nobody ever doubted—

that a being who can give any possession to another must at first have had that possession in his own hands? Is it not a waste of time to construct the conclusion that the former of the eye must himself have light, and that the inspirer of knowledge must himself be wise?

And truly, to the common mind this first impression would seem to be the only tenable one. It so happens, however, that the common mind is in this instance at variance with the view of modern scientific and philosophic systems.

The psalmist asks, "He that planted the ear, shall He not hear? He that formed the eye, shall He not see?" The scientific materialist answers, There is not the least necessity. Let it be observed that the scientific materialist has no more doubt than the most orthodox theist, that the ear must have been planted and that the eye must have been formed by *something*. What that something is he does not profess to know, but he expresses his idea of its working by the general term evolution. He has no objection whatever to say that the ear has been planted and the eye formed by the developing process of *Nature*. He is therefore at one with the theist in seeking a cause or antecedent for the planting of the ear and the forming of the eye. But where he differs from the theist is in the refusal to recognise the necessity that the giver of such intelligent organs as the ear and the eye should itself be intelligent. It is to him self-evident that these instruments of intellectual thought may have proceeded from a source of which the idea of thought is not predicable. The scientific materialist would not for an instant deny that there is design in nature; he admits that there is design in the actions of his own mind. But then he will not accept the doctrine that design must have come from design; Lange says in so many words that the purposeful has grown out of the purposeless. This is only, in other words, directly to reverse the psalmist's argument, and maintain that the ear may be planted by a power that is deaf, that the eye may be formed by a force that is blind.

Now at first sight it seems incredible that such a view should be held by any class of men. But if we look a little beneath the surface, we shall find that science is not wholly responsible for its promulgation, that in truth it rests upon a basis which is commonly accepted as much by the philosopher as by the scientist. It is almost universally held, alike by spiritualists and by materialists, that an effect has no resemblance to its cause. We are told again and again that there is no analogy whatever between a blow and the pain that follows it, between the vibration of the air and the sensation of music which succeeds it, between the image on the retina and the perception of light which flows from it. From this it is said to follow as the veriest truism, that the effect is not in any sense similar to that which produced it. Whether the conclusion follows from the premiss, we shall presently consider; but in the meantime we wish to point out that if this conclusion be true, agnosticism is the only rational belief in the universe. Once grant that the effect has no resemblance to its cause, and you have destroyed for ever not only the argument from design, but every other argument for the support of theism. Once grant that there is no analogy between that which is produced and that which has produced it, and, for all that you know to the contrary, every effect may be the result of its direct opposite. The materialist is then right in saying that life does not require life to account for its origin; if the effect has no resemblance to the cause, why should not spirit be the child of matter? The agnostic is then right in saying that the existence of design in me is no proof of the presence of design in that which produced me; if the effect has no resemblance to the cause, why should not the purposeful have grown out of the purposeless? The admission of this so widely accepted principle destroys at one blow the very possibility of faith, the very foundation of all religion.

On the other hand, if this position be denied, if it be held that the effect *has* a resemblance to the cause, agnosticism must of necessity cease to exist. Once grant that what exists in the product must have existed in the producer, and all argument is thenceforth at an end; religion has triumphed, and triumphed permanently. There is no longer any need of pursuing the argument from design, there is no longer any necessity for indulging in abstract speculation. The rankest materialist will admit that if the necessary resemblance of the effect to its cause could be established, materialism would, as a matter of course, cease to be. Human beings feel themselves to be in possession of intelligence; if it could be proved that the cause must resemble the effect, it would be proved that the cause of human beings was intelligent; there would be a direct affirmative to the question of the psalmist, "He that planted the ear, shall He not hear? He that formed the eye, shall He not see?"

It has always seemed to us a very singular thing that the principle here insisted on should have occupied so insignificant a place in the history of natural theology. We have had whole treatises on the argument from design; we have had bulky volumes on the argument *a priori;* we have had lengthy disquisitions on the traces of a providential government. These are all good, but none of them lies at the root of the matter. The root of the matter is the unanswered question of the psalmist: "He that planted the ear, shall He not hear? He that formed the eye, shall He not see?"—the question, in other words, whether there can exist an effect which has no resemblance to the cause of its being? On the answer to that question depends the validity of every other argument. If a negative answer be returned, what is the use of establishing the proof of design in nature? As we have already said, no one ever denies that design exists in *you*. The question, and the only question, is, whether design in you implies design in that which originated you? If the effect has no necessary resemblance to its cause, your proof of intelligence in nature is labour in vain. The real point of the difficulty has been touched by the old Jewish psalmist, when he desires to know whether an ear can be the product of aught but hearing, or an eye the offspring of aught but sight. If natural theology would reach the crucial point, it must go back to the principle involved in the question of the psalmist. Let the theologian retrace his steps beyond the outworks into the citadel. Let him leave in the meantime his argument from design, his argument *a priori*, his argument from the Providence of history, and let him go back to the ancient but still unanswered question of the psalmist—unanswered, that is, by scientific investigation. Let him confine his attention solely and earnestly to the principle involved in that question—the relation which subsists between an effect and its cause. If, as the result of long study and exhaustive induction, he shall succeed in establishing the position that their relation is one of resemblance, he shall have crowned apologetics with a triumph which all the united works on Christian evidence have failed to achieve, for he shall have placed it beyond all possible doubt that the Power lying at the basis of this universe is the force of an intelligent life.

The psalmist, it will be observed, never entertains a doubt as to the affirmative answer which must be returned to his question; he makes the inquiry in the manner of a *reductio ad absurdum*. Now the question is, Is this confidence of the psalmist an anachronism? We have already said that it is the common opinion both of scientists and philosophers that there is no necessary resemblance between an effect and its cause. But this does not make the psalmist's view an anachronism. Nothing can make an old view obsolete but a knowledge of contrary facts. The question is, Have there intervened since the days of the psalmist any new facts which have rendered it impossible to adhere to his opinion? or, Have we reached any interpretation of the old facts which militates against that opinion? That is the question we intend to consider in the present chapter. We do not seek here to establish a *proof* that the effect must have a resemblance to its cause; that is a task which would require a volume to itself, and would demand a more extensive knowledge of all departments of nature than we claim to possess. We here confine ourselves to the disproof of the negative. The whole motive of our present inquiry is to investigate whether the religious sentiment be an anachronism, whether it has been superseded by the facts of the new science. It is in this light alone, therefore, that we propose to view the present subject. The psalmist declares that an effect cannot exist which has no resemblance to its cause; we want to know whether the advance of modern investigation has made that declaration obsolete, whether the light of the new science has compelled us to revise the old conclusion, and so placed another barrier in the way of the religious sentiment.

There are three directions in which the conclusion of the psalmist has been assailed, three grounds on which it has been declared impossible to hold that the effect must necessarily have a resemblance to its cause. They are all grounds of experience, and as such they merit our closest attention. They may be comprehended under the names—everyday experience, chemical experience, and evolutionary experience.

Strangely enough, it is in the field of everyday experience that the sentiment of the psalmist has encountered its severest opposition. Obvious as the conclusion seems to be that an effect cannot proceed from something which is wholly unlike it, there are yet facts of common observation which appear on the surface to point to a contrary inference. It is on the ground of one of these everyday experiences that the psalmist's argument has met the ridicule of one of our greatest modern thinkers. Mr J. S. Mill, in speaking of the belief that an effect must resemble its cause, sarcastically asks whether the cook who made this hot soup must herself have been made of pepper. We were ourselves lately accosted by the same question in another form. In ventilating the views to which we are here giving publicity, we were interrupted by a gentleman's interrogation, whether his wife had any resemblance to the picture of a dog which she had just painted. The question came to us as a help, and threw back its light upon that of Mr J. S. Mill. We saw it to be a test case on which the whole fabric must rise or fall. Clearly there was no resemblance between the living woman and the painted dog, any more than there was any resemblance between the pepper in the soup and the nature of the cook. Was, then, the whole ship to be wrecked on this small rock, or was there an error somewhere in the statement of the question? Was there any point assumed in the question which was not really involved in it? If so, where did it lie?

A very brief reflection soon led us to the discovery that there was an error in the statement of the major premiss—the woman who painted this dog is the cause of the dog. Such a premiss, if accepted as valid, could certainly lead to only one conclusion—that the effect in this case was altogether unlike its cause. But a deeper observation makes it clear that the woman in this instance is not the cause of the painted dog. The cause of the painted dog is not the woman in herself, but the woman in the act of painting. The inward personality has very little to do with the matter; any other person would have done as well, provided he or she had performed the same physical process. Now, let us observe that the moment the matter is stated in this way, we get a complete reversal of our first impression. When the painted dog is referred to the act of the painter, so far from being unlike the cause which produced it, it will be found to be an exact copy of that cause, a direct transcript of the impression which has been made. The two elements to be taken into the account are the colour and the form, and each of them is explained, and only explained, on the principle of resemblance to the cause. The colour impressed on the canvas is the colour originally contained on the brush which communicated it; the form of the completed structure is the final result of those movements by which the hand of the artist guided itself into different spatial directions. It seems to us that there are more things in the universe than the painted dog which may be ultimately found to have their explanation in the same way. It is a favourite doctrine of mental philosophy that there can be no resemblance between things as they really are and things as we see them. If so, we shall be warranted in asking whether the forms of things as they really are, are the causes of those forms which we see; and if not, what are these causes? May it not be that the forms which we see are, like the form of the painted dog, the last results of those spatial directions which the forces of the brain traverse in conducting the processes of life? The question is one for the physiologist; we merely throw out the suggestion and pass on.

The illustration of the painted dog is exactly analogous to the illustration of Mr J. S. Mill, and as the result of examination it must share the same fate. He says that on the principle of resemblance between the effect and its cause, the cook who made the hot soup must herself have been made of pepper. We accept the conclusion, but we insist on a definition of terms. Mr Mill understands the cook to be the woman; clearly this is inadequate—the cook is the woman in action, and in that particular form of action called culinary. Looking at the matter in this light, we have no hesitation whatever in saying that pepper must have been in the cook's composition; it is one of the ingredients in the cause, the other ingredient being an active will. Meantime, what we have to observe is, that everything which has passed from the cause into the effect bears an exact resemblance in the latter to what it presented in the former. The pepper in the soup owes its origin to pepper outside the soup. There is more than that: whatever may be said of the principle of biogenesis in general, there is no doubt that in this instance the vital sensation of heat is the direct result of a preceding vital sensation of the same sort. If the pepper came into the soup by an act of cookery at all, and not by the force of a blind accident, it will be impossible to avoid the conclusion that the heat which I feel owes its origin to the mental feeling of the same heat in the cook's imagination, the mental feeling being itself, according to materialistic science, only a reproduction of the actual sensation. Here then, in this famous illustration of Mr Mill, we have a direct instance of the principle that an effect resembles its cause. We have an outward ingredient, called pepper, associated with an inward sensation, called heat, and each of them, as a matter of fact, is referable to a similar element. The pepper has its origin in the impartation of its own essence from without, and the sensation of heat, on the part of the recipient, owes its origin to the fact that the same sensation was at first experienced and afterwards imagined by the woman who made the soup.

Now, it will be found that in every instance in which the experience of everyday life has seemed to violate the argument of the psalmist, the cause of the seeming violation has been the same as in the famous illustration of Mr Mill. What is the reason that, at first sight, Mr Mill's illustration wears an appearance of plausibility? Why is it that, on a superficial view, it seems to establish the position that there is no necessary resemblance between an effect and its cause? The reason of the plausibility lies in this, that there is an assumed major premiss which is yet not expressed; if it were expressed, the validity of the reasoning would at once be questioned. Mr Mill says that there is no resemblance between the pepper in the soup and the woman who put it there; this is true and indisputable. But then Mr Mill takes it for granted that the woman is the sole cause of the pepper; he forgets that the act of *putting it there* counts for something in the transaction. The cook is with him simply the person; in any scientific statement of causality, she must be viewed as the person in action. The error of Mr Mill, therefore, is a logical error; it consists in attributing to the part of a cause the accomplishment of the whole. Now, in every case in which the commonplace experiences of life seem to lend a similar plausibility to the essential difference of effect and cause, it will be found on examination that there is a similar logical error at the root of the statement; in other words, that a part of the cause is taken for the whole. Take, for example, that instance adverted to above—the statement that there is no resemblance between the force which inflicts a blow and the pain which follows it. Of course there is no resemblance; no man, either ancient or modern, would maintain that there is.

But shall we conclude from this that there is no necessary resemblance between an effect and its cause? If we do, we are simply repeating the logical error of Mr Mill; we are assuming that the force which inflicts a blow is the cause of that pain which follows it. Now, it is certainly one of the causes, but only one. There is another important factor in the process, and that is—the existence of a sentient organism. We are popularly in the habit of thinking that the sentiency has been created by the blow; in point of fact, unless the sentient element be co-operative, there can be no pain at all. The force of the most ponderous blow descending on a wooden board will never produce pain, nor would it have any effect even on a human organism if the members of that organism were mortified. This is, of course, a truism; but it is one of those truisms which, in a discussion of this kind, are highly suggestive. To say that no force impinging on a dead body can communicate pain to that body is just, in other words, to say that life itself is required as one of the factors in the production of pain. It is quite unnecessary, therefore, to seek a resemblance between the striking force and the suffering impression, quite irrelevant to discover a difference between them. Whatever difference exists between the effect and that part of the cause under observation, is to be accounted for by the fact that there is another part of the cause which is not under observation, but which, were it only visible, would destroy the appearance of unlikeness between the thing produced and the agency of its production.

This leads us to consider the second of these classes of phenomena which appear at first sight to militate against the view of the psalmist; it is that which we have called chemical experience. It is alleged that in the sphere of chemistry two compounds can produce a third element which in its nature is distinctly different from either. If so, we shall be driven inevitably to the conclusion that the argument of the psalmist is untenable; that there is no necessity for a resemblance to exist between an effect and its cause—that the power which planted the ear need not hear, and that the force which formed the eye need not see. But is it so? To answer this question we do not require to examine a series of instances; we shall take a test case, a case on which modern science itself desires that the argument may stand or fall. The instance to which we allude is Professor Huxley's celebrated illustration derived from the supposed absence of an analogy between the substance called water and those elements of oxygen and hydrogen which compose it.[1] Professor Huxley wishes to show that there is no reason in the nature of things why the thing we call life should not have been originally produced by non-living matter. To support this view he adduces

[1] Lay Sermons, p. 149.

the instance of water, which is a product of the two chemical elements called oxygen and hydrogen, but which he avers bears no resemblance to these elements. He asks if there is any greater difference between the product called life and the material structure which forms its basis, than there is between the substance called water and the oxygen and hydrogen which constitute its composition. He says that in this latter case there is not a single analogy between the effect and its cause; and he asks with an air of triumph, why in the case of life and mind we should not be content to accept a similar absence of resemblance. If an element like water can proceed from elements so unlike it as oxygen and hydrogen gas, why should not the ear be planted by that which does not hear, and the eye formed by that which does not see?

Now, Professor Huxley has thrown down this case as a gantlet; he is willing to rest upon it the issue of the whole argument. We shall therefore accept it as a test case, and should we find that it does not bear out Professor Huxley's conclusion, we shall be warranted in inferring that no objection on the side of chemistry can be made to the faith of the psalmist. The simple question then is, Does the instance given by Professor Huxley bear out his own position? does the nature of the element called water prove by illustration that there is no necessary resemblance between an effect and its cause? Professor Huxley says that water differs essentially from the oxygen and hydrogen which compose it. We ask, Wherein does that difference consist? If it lie anywhere it must be in one or other of three things —either in the quantity, in the effective power, or in the appearance. Is the difference between water and the two elements which compose it a difference of quantity? Professor Huxley himself and every man of science in the world will strenuously maintain that it is not. It is the express doctrine of evolution that in the correlation of forces the quantities are exactly equivalent. The forces involved in each of the elements called oxygen and hydrogen are neither more nor less than the forces involved in that union of oxygen and hydrogen which forms water. So far, then, the effect is not only not dissimilar to the cause, but is the exact reproduction of the cause. Let us take, therefore, the second alternative. Is the effective power of water different in its quality from what we should predict the united effect of oxygen and hydrogen to be? Oxygen and hydrogen, when taken separately, have confessedly contrary properties: oxygen preserves flame; hydrogen explodes or extinguishes it. Let us consider now those relative proportions of the two elements which are necessary to the production of water. In order to produce water two volumes of hydrogen must be combined with one volume of oxygen; in other words, a double portion of the explosive or extinguishing element must be brought into contact with a single portion of the preserving element. What, then, should we naturally expect or predict from such a combination? Clearly that after the union of the two there would be an element in existence which would have the effect of extinguishing flame wherever it was applied to it, and yet of extinguishing it not with absolute instantaneousness, but as the result of an overcome resistance. Such is exactly the effect which as a matter of fact results from the application of water to fire: the fire is extinguished after a resistance more or less strong. The reason both of the extinction and of the struggle lies in the fact that the water is on both sides of the question. It contains within itself an element common to the fire, and therefore an element which if it stood alone would preserve the fire. But it does not stand alone. In addition to this force in common with the fire, the water contains another force of exactly the opposite tendency, a force which by its nature is opposed to the continuance of flame; and as the water possesses this second force in a double proportion to the former, there results a complete suppression of the first tendency and an ultimate extinction of the fire. Here again there is not only no contrariety between the effect and its cause, but a complete and unbroken harmony, a perfect resemblance between the effect produced with the two forces in combination, and the effect which must have been predicted from looking at the two forces in isolation with reference to such a union.

On two sides, therefore, we have been brought to one conclusion—that the illustration given by Professor Huxley, so far from proving his position, goes to establish a contrary position, the necessary resemblance between an effect and its cause. We have seen that whatever distinction exists between oxygen and hydrogen in their separation, and oxygen and hydrogen in their union, does not consist in a difference of quantity. We have seen that wherever the dissimilarity may lie between the elements in isolation and the elements in combination, it certainly does not lie in the fact that the elements in combination have a power which we could not have predicted from seeing them in isolation. One other alternative remains, and it is that on which Professor Huxley will probably base his case: it may be said, and it cannot be gainsaid, that when oxygen and hydrogen are united in the form of water, they present to the senses a totally different *appearance* from that which they have in separation. This is the most plausible point in Professor Huxley's case, because it is something which is instantaneously evident to the most common observation. When Professor Huxley speaks of the dissimilarity between this effect and its cause, his mind is mainly dwelling upon a dissimilarity of appearance. He is looking at water as he proposes to look at life—in

E

the light of a phenomenon addressed to the senses. If the phenomenon called water when addressed to the organs of sense presents so totally different an appearance from those phenomena called oxygen and hydrogen which caused it, why should not the element named life be also allowed to present an appearance totally unlike those materials which formed its being? Why should we not be entitled to say that as the appearance called water is a manifestation of oxygen and hydrogen, so the appearance called life is a manifestation of material protoplasm?

Such is Professor Huxley's reasoning, and it has in it an air of plausibility. But now, if we look deeper, we shall see that there is a flaw in the argument — nay, that there is precisely the same flaw which appeared in the reasoning of Mr Mill. Let us observe that throughout the whole train of Professor Huxley's argument there is the assumption of something whose truth is considered so self-evident that it is not only never proved, but never even stated. It is taken for granted that the peculiar appearance presented by water owes its origin to the combination of the two elements, oxygen and hydrogen. Now, so far from being self-evident, this is not the fact. The combination of oxygen and hydrogen is certainly a part of the reason why water has its peculiar appearance, but it is only a part, and therefore by itself it is as inadequate to explain the whole as if it had no connection with the process at all. Professor Huxley assumes that there are only two factors engaged in producing the appearance of water— oxygen and hydrogen. In reality there are three — oxygen, hydrogen, and the sensuous organism. It is the wildest delusion to imagine that in the appearance which water presents to the senses these senses themselves have no share ; on the contrary, they are the main factor in the production of the result. If two men come behind me and push me violently forward, there results from that combination of forces the manifestation of a third and quite different apparition—I am myself brought to the ground. But will it be said that this third phenomenon is entirely due to the combination of the two first forces ? Is it not clear that I myself am a most important factor in the production of my own fall ? The principle in Professor Huxley's illustration is precisely the same. The two forces, oxygen and hydrogen, are in combination to produce a result upon *me*, but in order to produce the result upon me I must myself co-operate with them. If I insist on shutting my eyes, the combination of the two forces will never present to my sight the appearance called water. No outward force and no combination of outward forces could ever generate a sensuous impression where there was not already in existence a sentient organism, and where that sentient organism was not already acting in harmony with them. If oxygen and hydrogen could produce the appearance of water in a bodily framework not already animated by life, Professor Huxley's illustration would be perfect, and the sentiment of the psalmist would be an anachronism. But in order to produce that appearance it is necessary that there should already be in existence a sentient principle which has proved itself otherwise capable of receiving visual impressions from the forces of nature, or of imparting to these forces its own visual envelopment. We have put the matter alternatively, because there are and probably will always be two distinct schools of thought on the subject of perception—one holding that the mind is clothed by nature from without, the other that the mind clothes nature from within. To our present subject it matters not. Whichever of the schools of thought we elect to follow—whether we say with Locke that the mind was originally a sheet of blank paper on which nature wrote, or whether we hold with Berkeley that what we call nature is itself but mind's handwriting on an unknown wall—we shall equally be driven to the conclusion that mind is an integral part in the causation of all phenomena. Whether it acts first or acts last it always acts energetically, and without its action the universe, as we know it, would cease to be. It is vain, therefore, for Professor

Huxley to attempt a parallel between the nature of life and the nature of water. Life itself is one of the ingredients in the production of water—nay, it is the main ingredient, for it is by this and by this alone that we reach that appearance of peculiarity and distinctiveness which seems to separate the water from those elements which constitute its structure.

We have now looked at this question from two sides; we have viewed it from the side of every-day experience, and we have considered it in the light of chemical knowledge. There remains yet another aspect in which we may regard it; we may contemplate it in its relation to the great principle of evolution itself. This is the field most commonly chosen by the professed scientific materialist. He tells us that as a matter of fact it has now been demonstrated that the law of the universe is a law of evolution, and he goes on to tell us that the law of evolution is a principle by which the higher comes out of the lower. He points as evidences of this demonstration to what we actually see in the world around us. He tells us that our own consciousness has been developed out of an unconscious germ-cell, that those lofty sensuous manifestations to which in their collective unity we give the name of mind were originally comprehended within the automatic movements of a piece of protoplasm. He tells us that what happens to the human embryo in each individual form, is precisely what has happened to the embryo of life in general. There must have been a time in which it began to be, and its beginning must have been like the beginning of the embryonic cell. It must have had its origin in forms analogous to those creatures which reveal simply movement and no more, and in which the passage from death into life has as yet not been detected on the part of the recipient. If, then, evolution teaches that as a matter of fact the higher grows out of the lower, the conscious out of the unconscious, the purposeful out of the purposeless, we are asked by what species of reasoning we shall attempt to show that there must exist a resemblance between the effect and its cause; by what argument we shall establish the position that the power which planted the ear must itself have been capable of hearing, and that the force which formed the eye must itself have been endowed with sight.

Such is the reasoning of the materialist based on the principle of evolution. But there is an error in the very heart of that reasoning—an error which will be admitted on reflection by the candid evolutionist himself; it lies in the materialist's definition of what evolution is. He defines it to be the principle by which the higher comes out of the lower. This is not the definition of evolution. Evolution is not the principle by which the higher comes out of the lower, but it is the principle by which the many come out of the one. An evolution may be an ascent from the lower to the higher, or it may be equally a descent from the higher to the lower; but it is neither the ascending nor the descending which makes it an evolution. The only thing which can entitle it to such a name, is the fact of its being a process whereby a single form of existence has been multiplied into many forms; whether the multiplication has been in an upward or in a downward direction, is quite another question. The nearest approach we can make to a description of what evolution is, will perhaps be reached by imagining the case of a very primitive community in which all professions are combined in the efforts of a single man; he is butcher, grocer, tailor, doctor, lawyer. In process of time the talents of the community will develop in different directions, and each man will start business in his own direction. The result will be that in a few years those offices originally discharged by a single man will be discharged by different men; there will be a distribution of those elements which at first were concentrated in unity. Yet in all this there is not really any generic advance from the lower to the higher; there is simply a disintegration of the one into the many. The elements which are ultimately shared throughout the community are not new discoveries; they have all already existed as the functions of one being. They are like the rivers of Paradise, which, in leaving their seat of unity, are parted into four heads, but which in the act of their partition have added nothing either to their quantity or to their essence.

If, then, evolution signifies essentially a disintegration of the one into the many, it is highly unscientific to assume before examination, that in any given case it must have been an ascent from the lower to the higher. To prove any process to be an evolution, we have only to prove that it has been a process whereby multiplicity has come from unity; but when we have reached this goal, the question will still remain in abeyance whether it has been a process upward or downward. That question cannot be solved by assumption; it can only be settled by patient investigation. We have no right, therefore, to say beforehand that the development of man is a process by which the conscious has grown out of the unconscious; we must try that question on other grounds. It is not difficult to see on what grounds it ought to be tried. Instead of assuming that consciousness is something which has been added in the course of development, the scientific method is to begin by asking whether anything else has been added. Let us in the meantime put consciousness on one side, and leave its origin an open question. Let us then direct our attention to those other elements which confessedly belong to the nature of man, and let us inquire whether these have or have not been added in the course of evolutionary development. If we shall find that any one of them has been so added, we shall require to give up the original pre-existence of consciousness, and along with it the argument of the psalmist. One negative instance is sufficient to overturn a whole train of inductive reasoning. If in the constitution of human nature there exists one element now which did not exist at the beginning, we shall have every reason to believe that the phenomena of consciousness are in a similar position. But if, on the other hand, we shall find that there is no physical element of man's present structure which did not exist at the first hour of his formation, if we shall discover that those organic materials which now constitute his completed development were present originally in that primitive process wherein his development began, we shall be justified in coming to the conclusion that the phenomena of consciousness also have been no after-growth of man's being, but have been themselves the main factors in bringing his being to perfection.

Now, at first sight it seems a startling and even an absurd question to ask whether the organic materials which are found in man's latest structure were originally present at the formation of that structure. It appears equivalent to asking whether the germ-cell is equal to the developed organism, whether the embryo is on a level with the full-grown man. Is it not transparent, previous to any argument, that the germ-cell is but a nucleus of the structure, that the embryo is but the first step in the organic ladder? And if so, how can it be asked whether the fully developed structure has added anything to the first nucleus of its formation? Is it not plain that it has added nearly everything to the elements of the germ-cell in which its life began? Undoubtedly it has; it has added nearly everything to the *germ-cell*, but the germ-cell is not the entire source of its original formation. The source of its original formation is the germ-cell in union with all nature. The doctrine of evolution does not hold—nay, does not admit—that the cause of the man is the embryo, or that the cause of the oak is the acorn. There was a time in which it was believed that the embryo contained the man, and the acorn the oak, in miniature. That doctrine has, in our century, been exploded. No man of science would now admit that the primitive elements of any structure existed originally in the nucleus of that structure. That every structure has an original nucleus will be denied by none, but it has in our days been ascertained that the original nucleus in any case forms a very insignificant factor in the development of the future plant or organism. The acorn could never produce the oak, the embryo could never produce the man; in order to reach their goal, each of them must enter into union with another and a more powerful factor. That factor is nothing less than the universe itself—that whole system of nature in which the primitive element of the future plant or animal is environed. In order to bring forth the oak, the acorn must be married to the material universe; the oak may have the acorn for its father, but it has united nature for its mother. Measured by the acorn in itself, the oak has vastly added to the materials of the original structure, for scarcely one of its later elements existed in the bosom of that structure. But though they existed not in the acorn, they were all present in the co-operative agency of nature; they were qualities of the mother, though not of the father. Amidst all the apparent addition, there has in reality been nothing added at all. Everything which did not at one time belong to the tree was at one time absorbed out of the air and sunshine. Not only has there been no addition in the direction of generic novelty; it is only in a qualified sense that we can affirm any addition in the direction of comparative intensity. To say that the effect cannot transcend the cause, is not merely to say that the absolutely new cannot come out of the old; it is to say that the perfect cannot come out of the imperfect. If the imperfect can of itself produce a form nearer to perfection, the principle of causality is as much transcended as if the old could produce the absolutely new. The developed man is vastly nearer to perfection than the embryonic germ-cell which formed the nucleus of his being; but we have seen that this nucleus is not the sole cause of his being. What prevents it from being the sole cause of his development is just the fact of its imperfection. There is an element in the developed man which is not present in the embryonic germ. Not being present in the embryonic germ, evolutionists conclude that at the first formation of man's being it must have been present elsewhere; elsewhere, accordingly, they have sought for it, and have found it in nature. Why have the evolutionists sought for the cause of human development outside as well as inside the germ? Why have they not been content to say that the imperfect embryo has produced the comparatively perfect man? Simply because the evolutionists themselves, whatever some of them may hold in theory, cannot admit in practice that the less can ever make the greater, that the part can ever generate the whole. Accordingly, it has become to them clear that the elements of man's materially developed structure are in no sense new elements, that the forces of man's physically organised being are in no sense new forces. They are merely readaptations, redistributions, readjustments, the entrance into new combinations, of things which in their isolated state existed long before in equal perfectness.

Such is the doctrine of evolution itself on this important and far-reaching question. It is not something advanced by the theologian as an argument against the modern theory of development; it is itself an integral part of that theory. Every evolutionist, whether materialist or spiritualist, atheist or theist, is agreed in asserting that the physical elements which compose any developed structure were originally present at the formation of that structure. They were not all nor even most of them present in the germ-cell, but those which were not in the germ-cell were supplied by external nature. To destroy this doctrine would be to destroy evolution at a blow, for it is a distinctive principle of evolution that no new element can be added to the original system of nature. The argument, therefore, begins to narrow itself. On the verdict of evolution itself, we have arrived at the conclusion that whatever physical elements exist now in any developed structure, must have existed beforehand at the formation of that structure. The question is, Is there to be one exception to the rule? There is an element in every organism whose origin presents a mystery to the eyes of all; it is the thing called life. Whether it be a thing physical or spiritual, is a question that will be differently answered by the materialist and the intuitionist. We shall not here dispute the point; it is irrelevant to our present purpose. What is relevant to our present purpose is to observe that the argument now in hand is of equal weight whether we adopt the view of the materialist or intuitionist, whether we decide to say that life is a very subtle form of matter, or prefer to call it a distinct and independent essence. We shall hereafter have occasion to estimate the relative probabilities of these views; meantime we shall assume, for the sake of the argument, that the materialist is right. We shall say that life is only the latest fruit of the physical tree, only the last and most refined product of the elements of outward nature. The question then comes to be this: Is this physical element which we call life to be the only physical element in nature whose phenomena and manifestations are altogether unlike the source from which they come? We have seen that in every other case, evolution itself being the judge, we have simply a distribution and collocation of old manifestations into new orders of arrangement; is this to be the one solitary instance in which the new distribution is to produce an effect so novel as to be, in the strictest sense, equivalent to a new creation? We ask the question in the interest of evolution itself; nor is it we who ask it for the first time. Why is it that Professor Huxley, after reducing everything to protoplasm, winds up by suggesting that protoplasm may not be what it seems? Why is it that Professor Tyndall,[1] after bringing all

---

[1] See Belfast address.

things within the circle of the material, declares that the common parentage from matter is inexplicable unless matter itself contain the promise and potence of life? Why is it that Professor Clifford,[1] after repudiating all theological conceptions, has referred the ultimate origin of things not to a set of physical forces, but to a series of sentient impressions or feelings? Why is it that Professor Haeckel,[2] after launching the thunderbolts of his wrath against every form of dualism, has declared that all matter has also a mental side? In each and all of these cases the reason is the same. It is because these men perceive that if matter be from the beginning the opposite of what we call life, the existence of life at the end is a creation out of nothing. It is because they see that to admit the rise of life from elements which had in them no original germ of the vital principle, is to deprive evolution itself of that basis of continuity on whose lines alone it can work. That is the ground on which the evolutionists of our day have been driven, in other words and in another form, to assert the self-same teaching of the psalmist, that the power which planted the ear must hear, and that the principle which formed the eye must see. If that teaching of the psalmist be in our days no longer valid, if it be one of those

[1] See an essay "Of Things as they are," in Sir Frederick Pollok's collection.
[2] See preface to his 'History of Creation.'

things which evolution has superseded, and science has rendered an anachronism, our evolutionists have given themselves useless trouble in seeking to find in matter the promise and the potence of life. Why should life have either a promise or a potence? If there is no need to seek any resemblance between an effect and its cause, there is surely no need to seek any premonition of the spiritual in the material. If that which makes one thing the cause of another is simply the fact of its antecedence, it is highly irrelevant to search in the antecedent for a promise or potence of the consequent. The fact that modern science does so search is itself deeply significant. It shows that in the view of evolutionists, and within the domain of evolution, we have not emerged from that ancient necessity of thought expressed in the question of the psalmist—the necessity to find in the cause a prefiguration of that which it produces. It reveals to our modern civilisation that with all its vaunted advance it has not even scientifically emancipated itself from the power of those primitive intuitions which regulated the life and the belief of earlier days, and that the instinct is as strong in science as it was in the Judaic religion, which prompted the mind of the psalmist to ask, "He that planted the ear, shall He not hear? He that formed the eye, shall He not see?"

We have seen, indeed, one curious attempt to refute this principle by the weapons of theology itself.

It occurs in one passage of a book written in the interest of evolution with much power and ability—Fiske's 'Cosmic Universe.' What Mr Fiske says is in effect this: Carry out your principle of the necessary resemblance between an effect and its cause, and see where it will land you. You feel intelligence in yourself, and you conclude that the cause which produced you must also be intelligent; you attribute to the Deity that which you perceive to be the noblest part of you. But why do you not say that because you are possessed of a body, the being who created you must also be a body? If you could imagine a piece of matter gifted with a momentary intelligence sufficient to inquire into the cause of its own existence, would it not be natural for that piece of matter to say, "I am material, therefore God must be material"? You would not accept the conclusion of this hypothetically endowed piece of matter, and yet in rejecting it you are rejecting the whole principle of your argument, the necessary resemblance between an effect and its cause. It seems very easy to infer that He who planted the ear must hear, and that He who formed the eye must see, because sight and hearing are to you the types of noble things whose analogies you are not unwilling to attribute to the Deity. But the ear itself would have an equal right to say that the power which created it must be an ear; the eye would have an equal right to affirm that the cause which formed it must be an eye. Your reason for rejecting the latter conclusion is simply your belief that matter is something degraded, which, therefore, you are not entitled to attribute to the Deity. But you must either accept your principle throughout, or abandon it altogether. If it be a principle that the effect must necessarily and at all times have a resemblance to its cause, then must you attribute materialism to God as well as spirituality and intelligence; if you refuse to seek the origin of materialism in something analogous in the nature of God, you are bound logically to reject the validity of the psalmist's argument that the planter of the ear must hear, and that the former of the eye must see.

Now in all this specious reasoning there is a glaring assumption. It is taken for granted from the outset that a piece of matter, as we know it, is something different from intelligence, and therefore something which on the psalmist's principle requires a different origin from intelligence. It is, on the contrary, a notorious fact that a piece of matter, as we know it, is neither more nor less than a form of intelligence. We say, "as we know it;" what it is in itself we cannot tell, and philosophers have always been divided as to whether its ultimate nature be real or ideal. But as to the appearance which it presents to us, there is not and never has been any difference of opinion at all. All of every school are agreed that whatever the piece of matter be in itself, it is, as known to us, only a series of sensations bound together by an act of thought. Its colour, its shape, its size, its hardness, its softness, are known to me simply as affections of my senses, and are perfectly inconceivable by me apart from the existence of a thinking mind. It cannot be too clearly kept in view that in the judgment of all scientists as well as of all philosophers, on the admission alike of Christian, theist, pantheist, agnostic, and materialist, the objects which we call physical are, as known to us, simply the manifestations of that which we term spirit. What appearance they may have outside the realm of spirit we shall never be able to know, but we know beyond all controversy that all which we see and hear and touch is simply a mental manifestation. We who believe in an ultimate principle of intelligence, and who ground our faith in that principle on the necessity for a resemblance between the effect and its cause, can have no difficulty whatever in finding the origin of matter in the nature of God. If matter is to us simply a manifestation of mind, it seems natural and even necessary to conclude that it has always been a manifestation of mind. What do we mean by attributing to God the fact of creation? Not merely that at some remote period of the past He called into being the visible system which we now behold—a conception which, if it stopped there, would leave us but half a God. What we mean by calling God the Creator is not that creative power was once one of His attributes, but that it is *always* one of His attributes. The creative power of God is a manifestation of Himself. The visible lives within the invisible; it is already to the spirit of the universe what it becomes to the spirit of man. Creation, all that we know of creation, exists in our thought—exists as a spiritual effect; where shall we look for a resembling cause? Where else can we look than to the recognition of the great belief that the creation which now exists in our thought existed eternally in the thought of God?

In the recognition of that belief the presence of the material universe shall become not a denial but a corroboration of the psalmist's faith, "He that planted the ear, shall He not hear? He that formed the eye, shall He not see?"

CHAPTER IV.

THE PSALMIST'S VIEW OF THE ORIGIN OF LIFE.

PSALM xxxvi. 9.

THE great scientific search of the nineteenth century is to elude the guardianship of the cherubim and the flaming sword, which, according to old tradition, keep the secret of the origin of life. Every step in the progress of evolution has been a step taken by science with the express purpose of unmasking this secret—of penetrating, if possible, beyond the environment of things into that inner court of the tabernacle which contains their unknown essence and hides their undisclosed mystery. Darwinism, in attempting to find a common origin for the plant, the animal, and the man, was really seeking to minimise the difference between the material and the immaterial; and the systems which have succeeded Darwinism in attempting to find a common origin for the man, the animal, the plant, and the earth on which they dwell, have sought to obliterate that difference altogether in the interest of an underlying unity.

Now the search for unity is a noble thing; it is the true aim of science and the highest goal of philosophy. We shall go far wrong, however, if we imagine for a moment that it owes its existence either to science or to philosophy; it is older than both. It finds its highest manifestation and receives its most perfect illustration in the religion of the Jewish commonwealth and in the sentiments of the Jewish prayer-book. The leading aim of the Israelitish nation was identical with the leading aim of modern science; it was the reference of all things to a principle of unity. Modern science, indeed, is more than a reference; it is an attempt to trace the unity. Judaism made no such attempt; it would have deemed it a vain and even a presumptuous task. But in spite of the distance in relative culture and development, Judaism aspired to do that very thing which modern science is seeking to achieve—to find a principle in the universe which may ultimately be recognised as the source of all things. Modern science searches for that principle laboriously and by slow degrees; Judaism approached it at a bound, and refused to analyse the steps by which it had found it. Instead of beginning with multiplicity and tracing the many up to the one, it began by postulating the one and tracing its influence down to the many. No scientific investigator of our age is more opposed to dualism than was the Jew. His whole life consisted in resting the universe on a single centre; any other thought, any other possibility, would have been to him a sentence of death. "The Lord our God is one Lord," was the main article of his creed and practice. The unity which he attributed to the object of his worship was not simply a pre-eminence over religious things; it was a centrality in the affairs of the world itself. The Alpha and the Omega of his belief lay in the one word Theocracy; God was all in all. He reigned not only without a rival, but without a second. Agencies to which the pious theist of our day gives the name of secondary causes, were to him as such non-existent. He did not deny their mediation, but he emphatically denied their co-operation. He admitted the influence of the winds, but he said that the winds were God's messengers; he admitted the strength of the fire, but he said that its flame was God's minister. When he had once adopted this principle as his standard, he never for a moment halted, never hesitated, never shrank from carrying out its conclusions into every region of human observation. He would not say with the Parsee that God was the cause of the light and the Devil the cause of the darkness; he insisted on finding for the darkness a place within the circle of light; he asked in so many words, "Shall there be evil in a city, and the Lord hath not done it?" What the pious theist of our day would call a divine permission, the Jew thought of as a divine decree; to him the very passiveness of God was active, and the determination to allow was equivalent to the command to be. The religion of the Jew was like the scientific faith of the nineteenth century, a protest against the admission that any event of life could be isolated from the chain of law, and on the incorporation of every event within that chain he meditated day and night.

Now let us here ask, What is the precise difference between the faith of the ancient Jew and the faith of the modern scientific materialist? Both are at one in seeking a principle of ultimate unity to which all objects and events may be referred. But the difference lies here: To the modern materialist life is one of those objects or events for which a principle of unity is to be sought; to the ancient Jew life was itself that principle of unity through which all other things were to be explained. This article of Jewish faith is clearly brought out in the text which we have prefixed to the beginning of this chapter: "With Thee is the fountain of life." Let it be observed that the psalmist does not mean to attribute to God the *origin* of life; he would have emphatically denied that life had any origin. His fundamental position is not that God created life, but that life is itself the nature of God, and therefore uncreated. It flows from Him as the stream flows from the fountain, yet the stream is of the same substance with the fountain; it is simply the diffusion into a new direction of what has already existed in concentrated unity. Even so the psalmist teaches that life is but a stream, a stream whose waters are not created but derived, and the source of whose derivation is an eternal fountain. This is the reason of that expression which is so constantly appearing in the aspirations of the Jewish prayer-book, "The living God." So far from looking upon life as something which is special and peculiar to organised beings, the psalmist would not have admitted that it is a necessary property of organisation at all. He held it to be the necessary property of one Being, and one alone—that Power which presides at the centre of the universe. He called this Power living, not merely to indicate that it was personal and intelligent, but to emphasise the fact that it alone lived by necessity. He expressed by anticipation that thought to which one of his own countrymen in far-distant years gave utterance when he declared that "in Him was life, and the life was the light of men." To us, indeed, the manner in which the fourth evangelist has spoken of the origin of life has always appeared very striking, and singularly characteristic of the national faith. He attributes to the divine Logos the work of creation, but he does so in very pointed language: "Without Him was not anything made that was made." It is customary to read the latter clause as a redundancy; this is not our opinion. The evangelist, in our view, meant to say that by the divine Logos everything was made *which required to be made*. But he clearly implies that there was something which did not require to be made, something already in existence which only needed to be utilised, and he does not leave us long in doubt what that something was. In the very next verse he says: "In Him was life, and the life was the light of men." Other things were created *by* Him but life was eternally *in* Him; He was the fountain of life. Life, being an eternal portion of His nature, was something which had no need to be created, and therefore it is presented by the evangelist as an exception to those "all things" which the divine Logos made. In making that exception the evangelist is at one with the spirit of his country. He is in harmony with that ancient tradition which saw, in the first movement of life in the waters, the very breath of the spirit of God; in unison with that religious sentiment which inspired the psalmist to proclaim that the fountain of life was the life of the Eternal. To the psalmist and to the evangelist alike, the researches of modern science, even did they issue in discovery, would have given no alarm. They would not have been startled by what is now called an act of spontaneous generation, any more than the writer of Genesis was startled by the boldness of his own statement that the earth brought forth the moving creature that has life. The writer of Genesis, the writer of the Psalms, and the writer of the fourth Gospel are too intent upon the Power from which life flows to attach much importance to the channel *through* which it flows. To them, as to the religious consciousness of their nation, there is no humiliation in the process of tracing man back to the dust of the ground, for they regard that beginning itself as but the end of a higher process—the action and the inspiration of the Spirit of God.

But for us the main question is, Is this sentiment an anachronism? Is it one of those modes of thought which are doomed to be dissipated with advancing light? Is it able to stand the test of that scientific investigation which has become the pre-eminent heritage of this nineteenth century? One thing, at the outset, is clear, and deserves to be carefully noted; there is no alternative on this matter between the view of the psalmist and the view of the scientific materialist. Either life is itself the fountain of life, or the fountain of life is matter—that which has no life. There is no middle course possible between the belief in a literally spontaneous generation, and the belief that life has never been generated at all. We must either stop short at some primitive form of matter and say, The vital spark had its origin here; or we must be content to assume that the vital spark had no origin anywhere—that, in fact, it has been eternal. If we take this latter course, two roads are open to us. We may say that the vital spark has been propagated from parent to offspring through an endless series of generations, or we may say that it had its eternal home in the being of one supreme Intelligence. It is, of course, possible to hold both these views at once; we might believe simultaneously in an eternal God and an eternal series of generations, but in this case the fountain of life is God and not the generations. We are not here discussing the relative probability of these two hypotheses. What we want to point out is this, that whichever of the roads we choose to follow, will bring us substantially to the psalmist's conclusion—life is the fountain of life. Whether we look upon that life as something originally concentrated in a single being, or whether we prefer to regard it as diffused through an infinite series of beings throughout endless time, we are alike agreed in holding that the source of present life is life eternal, that the fountain from which flows the vitality of every living form is itself a living fountain without beginning of years.

There is another preliminary consideration which should not be left out of account in a review of this subject, and it is this: every plausible attempt which modern science has made to find the fountain of life in the order of material nature, has ended unconsciously in adopting the conclusion of the psalmist. This may seem a somewhat sweeping assertion and even a paradox, but we think it will be borne out by the facts. There have been in our days several important efforts to find an origin for life identical with the origin of all other things. As representing this tendency, we may instance in our own country the names of Professor Huxley and Professor Tyndall, and in Germany, the name of Professor Haeckel. In relation to the first two, it is quite notorious that they ultimately reach a common origin for things by altering at the last moment their own conception of matter. Tyndall, after reducing everything to a fire-cloud, declares that it would be positive insanity to believe in the parentage from that fire-cloud, provided it is conceived to be what it appears to be. In order to accept it as the original germ out of which life sprang, it is necessary to hold that the fire-cloud itself was in its deepest essence, not material, but spiritual, and contained the promise and potence of that life which it generated. When we turn to Professor Haeckel, we seem at first sight to be confronted with a more uncompromising opponent. He declaims vehemently against the tendency of spiritual thinkers to see a dualism in the universe. He professes to treat the existence of consciousness in man very much in the light of a *lusus naturæ*. He regards it as a kind of abnormal growth or development which instituted a special and unique manifestation in one department of the universe. But he asks what right man has to project this consciousness of his into the past. He professes to show that everything else in nature can be traced back to what he calls a principle of monism. What right has this little insignificant thing, called consciousness, coming as it does late upon the stage, and occupying an infinitesimal portion of that stage, to set up its puny self as coeval with the eternity of matter? It is at present the one solitary element which seems to resist the tendency to a materialistic origin; is it not the highest presumption for it to hold that an existence, apparently but of yesterday, has been present at the birth of worlds?

This is an unpromising beginning. But when we come to the end of Professor Haeckel's investigations, we are struck by the fact that the hands of Esau have issued in the voice of Jacob. The preface of a book is always the latest part of an author's work, and therefore the statement of a preface may be accepted as the last word of the writer. Now, in the preface to his 'History of Creation,' Professor Haeckel, as we have already seen, makes the assertion that all matter has a mental side. We believe he never uttered a more profound truth. It is quite certain that the dualism which exists between the outward world and the inward human consciousness, so far from being something special and peculiar to the nature of man, finds a precise analogy throughout all the works of nature. There is as great a dualism, as inexplicable a chasm, between the primitive elements of force and matter, as there is between the latest elements of subject and object. Every piece of matter is a compound of two worlds, a world without and a world within. Its outer world is what we call its materialism; its inner is the force which keeps it together. How these two elements are united, no man can tell; the only points clear are, that they *are* united and that they are seemingly contrary. No man can understand how matter should produce force, for it is the nature of matter to continue in its present condition, whatever that may be. If at rest, it would remain at rest for ever unless moved from without; if in motion, it would never come to rest unless impeded on its way. On the other hand, it is equally impossible to conceive how force can generate matter, for force itself is simply motion, and motion demands that there be something to be moved. Here is a dilemma exactly analogous in its nature to that seeming contradiction of matter and spirit which meets us partially in the animal and fully in the man, and Professor Haeckel could not have expressed himself more happily or more truly than he has done in the aphorism, that all matter has a mental side.

But the wonder in this case is that Professor Haeckel of all men should have ever arrived at or admitted this truth. He has been telling us from the beginning that monism is the law of the universe, and he has written his book with the express view of establishing that position. And now, at the end of his book, and at the summing up of all his investigations, he comes forward with a position exactly the contrary of that which it has been his aim to demonstrate; he tells us in the last result that the law of the universe is not monism but dualism, and that matter has a side allied to mind. Has it, then, all come to this? Has all this vaunted effort after unity issued only in the affirmation which is accepted even by the vulgar, that there is an eternal dualism in the nature of things; that in every movement of the natural universe we are compelled to assume the co-operation of something which transcends the ordinary notions of matter? It is not here our object, however, to criticise Professor Haeckel for his want of consistency; we have to do, not with his book, but with his conclusion. For that conclusion, we have to thank him; it is a concession from the camp of materialism. The most pronounced advocate which this century has produced of a materialistic tendency in modern science, has reached, at the last step of his analysis, the conception of a matter which on one side of its nature is allied to spirit. What is this but in other words to say that the conclusion of modern science is but a reiteration of the conclusion reached by that religious sentiment which declared, three thousand years ago, that the fountain of life could be life alone?

We have now cleared the ground for the consideration of this subject. We have seen that there are only two alternatives which are open to discussion—the hypothesis that life has been eternal, and the hypothesis that life has been generated by matter. Which of these is the view most consonant with the results of modern science? It is commonly assumed that the tendency of modern science has been to give currency to the belief in the possibility of a spontaneous generation. The truth is, it is to modern science that we are indebted for any doubt that has been cast upon that belief. The doctrine of spontaneous generation was, up to the close of the seventeenth century, held by all classes, both amongst the vulgar and amongst the learned. The belief that certain inferior forms of life could spring from forms which were not living, was not only held by our ancestors, but it was held without alarm. The reason, however, of the comparative unconcern is not difficult to find. To a man of the seventeenth or eighteenth century there could be nothing alarming in the suggestion that the lowest forms of life might have a purely physical origin, for he firmly believed that there was a great gulf fixed between his own human life and all animal forms whatsoever. But to the man of the nineteenth century it is all the reverse. The doctrine of evolution is in the air, and the doctrine of evolution distinctly teaches that there is no possibility of a gulf between any forms of life. Let the primitive form once be accounted for, and evolution will account for all the rest. Only explain how the earliest vital impulses began to manifest themselves, and the modern doctrine of development will trace the whole windings of the stream, from its first small and insignificant flow to its expansion into the ocean of human intelligence. It is easy to perceive what a vast difference the belief in spontaneous generation must make to men holding such a creed. To one who believes that the race of man is distinct from all other races, the controversy between a Pasteur and a Bastian must be a subject rather of curiosity than of solicitude; if my origin is from above, it can matter little to me that certain fungi have revealed an origin from beneath. But if I have become partaker of the scientific spirit of the nineteenth century, if I have come to the conclusion that the life of the human race was once the life of the fungi, the controversy of a Pasteur and a Bastian becomes to me a matter of death and life. If the fungus be proved to have had its origin from beneath, I too, in accordance with the spirit of evolution, have been placed amongst inferior things. It matters not how many and how devious be the stages that have intervened between the first production of the primitive life and the culmination of that life in me; the question of origin centres purely in the first production, and if that production has been a growth out of dead matter, then is dead matter the author of my being.

We have thought it right to emphasise this point, in order to show wherein consists the materialistic danger of the nineteenth century. It is popularly thought to consist in the advent of new facts; it really lies in the application of old facts to the doctrine of evolution. The facts supposed to point in the direction of materialism have been rather diminished than increased by the science of our century. What has given a materialistic tendency to this science is the promulgation of that doctrine of development which has put old things in a new light, and rendered formidable what at one time was innocent and indifferent.

So far then as experiment is concerned, the scientific influence of the nineteenth century has been, from the materialistic standpoint, rather reactionary than progressive, has tended rather to diminish than to augment the alleged number of those instances in which the science of the past thought to detect the evidence of spontaneous generation. In spite of this, however, it remains none the less true that the science of the nineteenth century has amongst its votaries a larger number of professed materialists than the science of any preceding age. We have seen that the cause of this is not the discovery of any additional fact which points in the direction of materialism; the tendency, on the contrary, exists in the very midst of the confession that every new experiment has tended more and more to discredit the evidence for spontaneous generation.[1] What is the ground of this paradox? If the majority of our leading scientists are agreed in holding that actual experiment has failed to establish one well-authenticated case of spontaneous generation; if they have thrown discredit upon conclusions which were once received as undoubted facts, and which, if accepted as facts, would make for materialism,—why is it that the tone of these same scientists is, in spite of their candour, more pronouncedly materialistic than the tone of their predecessors? The question is one which demands strict investigation. It seems to us that the paradox points to a fact which has not commonly been observed by apologetic writers. It is usually taken for granted that the question of the existence or non-existence of spontaneous generation is to be determined by the discovery or by the failure to discover the procession of living germs from dead matter. Very naturally, therefore, apologetic writers are surprised to find, that in spite of the failure to discover such germs, scientific materialism is more rampant than ever. But the truth is, that whether spontaneous generation be true or false, it does not need to wait for its confirmation upon the

[1] See Professor Huxley's article "Evolution" in ninth edition of 'Encyclopædia Britannica.'

discovery of any such germs. To the science of our century the evidence for spontaneous generation is not a fact of experiment, but an alleged fact of experience. The materialist of our day offers to give every man an individual and personal proof that life can spring from material forces. He offers to give him that proof without leading him into any laboratory, without showing him any instruments, without asking him to witness any experiments. He proposes simply to lead him into his own consciousness, and to bid him examine the process of his own life. This is in our day the real stronghold of the doctrine of spontaneous generation. Instead of introducing us to a series of intricate experiments which can only be observed by a scientific eye, and can only be tested by a scientific culture, we are ushered into the commonplace chamber of our own experience, and are told to observe those facts of daily life which he that runneth may read. Let us try briefly to explain the nature of these alleged facts.

In order to do so, we shall endeavour to throw ourselves into intellectual sympathy with the materialist; we shall try to be impressed as he is with the force of the argument he designs to put before us. What the materialist then says is this: Some ten, twenty, or thirty years ago you were a child; now you are a man. Here are two commonplace facts of your experience, the observation of which requires no culture. Now I ask you to put together these facts, to consider as a matter of experience what is the precise point of contrast between the life which you now have as a man and the life which you once had as a child. Does it not lie just in this, that you have now more life than you had then? Is not the difference between the years of your childhood and the years of your maturity just the fact that in the interval there has been added to your being a new stream of vitality? But now observe what is implied in this: is it anything else than spontaneous generation? Where has the more life come from? If there has been an addition to the original vital stream of your being, to what is that addition to be referred? To what can it be referred but to the correlation of the material forces? If new life has entered into you in the interval between the child and the man, it can only be because new life has been generated by the action of matter upon your organism; and what is this but spontaneous generation? You tell me that I have failed to produce one well-authenticated instance of a new germ of life being generated from dead matter. It is true I have so failed, but why? Simply because, in order to produce life, there must exist beforehand the conditions of life. If you could bring into one focus all those material conditions which are necessary to vital being, there would be no difficulty in showing an instance of spontaneous generation. In the case of organic germs we cannot get these preliminary conditions, but in the case of your own organism we can. The body which you had as a child had in it all the conditions necessary to the existence of life. What was the result? It was not only able to keep alive the life which it had, but it was able to add life more abundantly. It was able to generate out of mere material elements, out of food and air and sunshine, out of forces which are popularly called physical, a life identical with its own, and harmonious with the law of its being. What further proof do you require of the possibility—nay, of the reality —of spontaneous generation?

We have tried to give this argument all the force we can. If we remember rightly, we first met with it in the writings of Dr Maudsley, and it made at the time a great impression on us. It seemed to us that the whole question was rested in a test case, in a manner which could be easily verified by every man's experience, and whose verification or disproof ought not to occupy much time. A deeper reflection has led us to a different conclusion. It will be found, we think, that this seemingly simple test case is really a syllogism consisting of three propositions, every one of which is taken for granted, and every one of which is, to say the least, very doubtful. The syllogism may be put thus: You have more life as a man than you had as a child; there is no other source from which your new life could have come than the physical forces of matter; therefore the physical forces of matter have spontaneously generated that life which has been added to your original being.

Of course it is evident that if the first and second propositions are proved, the third must also be true. But in order to test the value of this syllogism it will be necessary to consider each proposition by itself. We propose, therefore, to begin with the third—the assertion that matter is the cause of that alleged addition to our original life which intervenes between the child and the man. We shall leave the question meantime in abeyance whether there has or has not been such an addition. We shall confine ourselves simply to the undoubted fact that there is a vast difference in development between the man and the child, reserving all judgment as to what constitutes that difference. The question now before us is whether the difference between the child and the man is something which has been brought about, or which ever could be brought about, by the agency of matter alone. The materialist has referred us to our own experience; to our own experience, therefore, let us go. Let us see whether the laws of human thought would naturally lead us to the conclusion that the difference between childhood and manhood can be produced by the unaided influence of the forces called physical.

Let us suppose that there were put into our hands, with the express purpose of testing this point, the life of a very young child. Let us suppose that we were asked for the benefit of physical science to make the life of this child an experiment. The problem would be to discover whether it would develop from childhood to maturity through the sole agency of matter. To work out this problem, we should therefore, from the beginning, studiously exclude from the child's development every other influence besides matter. Let it be observed that the word "matter" would itself here require to be used in a very restricted sense. We would not be at liberty to include the phenomena of light and sound amongst the permitted influences, because the phenomena of light and sound in the moment of their perception cease to be material, and become influences of the spirit. The truth is, in order to test our problem we would require to limit the developing influences of the child to the simple participation in food and air, these being the nearest approach we have to distinctively bodily influences. Let us, therefore, limit our hypothetical child to the use of these two elements. Let us ordain that, from this day forth, it shall be incarcerated within walls which shall not even reveal the shadows of Plato's cave. Let us command that it shall be kept studiously from the contact with every ray of light, and the communion with every note of sound. Let us deny it the fellowship of all comrades, the perusal of all books, the access to all newspapers—everything, in short, but that which is essential to the maintenance of present life and the growth of bodily strength. The question is, At the end of the intervening years what will be the difference between the child and the man? There will clearly be a difference in physical strength, physical size, physical proportions; and this difference will certainly imply that something has been added to the child since the day of its incarceration. But this something will be precisely such a thing as could be added by matter; in point of fact, it will be found to consist exclusively of the forces called material. No man has ever denied that these forces exist in a larger measure in the man than in the child, and no man has ever disputed that the cause of their increase is materialism. But it is not the increase of these forces which has ever been supposed to constitute the difference between the man and the child. That which constitutes the difference between them lies in the phenomena of consciousness. Whether the difference amounts to an *increase* of consciousness is not here the question; it is not denied on any hand that the man is a vast development beyond the child, and it is doubted by no one that what marks the distinction between them is mental superiority. Now let us ask, Will this crucial point of distinction appear in the instance before us? Will the consciousness of the child after its years of incarceration be one whit superior to the consciousness of the child before it was incarcerated? We have admitted that in bodily strength it will have become a man; will it have become a man in mind? Will it be one stage nearer than it was in its earliest years to that which constitutes our ideal of manhood? The universal answer of every intelligent mind will be "No." It is almost a truism to say that in the circumstances we have supposed, a child would remain for ever a child, which is only in other words to say that there would in this instance be no increase in that element which distinguishes between the child and the man.

But now, what is implied in this admission? Clearly that matter alone is not adequate to produce the difference indicated. Matter in this instance has had a fair trial; it has been the only agency allowed to have any share in the child's development. Everything has been excluded but bread, with the view of determining the question whether man can live by bread alone, whether that life of higher reason which we call distinctively the age of manhood could ever be produced at all were matter the sole agent at work. The common-sense of the observer has been constrained to give a negative answer, has been forced to confess that in the circumstances here indicated no lapse of time could effect the change from the child into the man. The conclusion is irresistible that, whatever part matter may have in the ordinary production of that change, it cannot have the sole part; it has been unable to effect it alone, and therefore it can only effect it through the co-operation of other influences.

So much then for the third proposition — the assertion that matter is the cause of the additional life which is supposed to intervene in the passage from childhood into maturity. We come now to the second proposition, which asserts that if there be more life in the man than in the child, there is no other source but matter from which the addition could come. Now it is quite plain that this is an assumption; it assumes that matter is the fountain of life. There is clearly another alternative which, whether it be accepted or not, cannot be put aside as non-existent. If the question before us had ever suggested itself to the mind of the psalmist, he would have answered it by saying that the additional life which the man possesses over the child is the result of a fresh stream of existence which is perpetually issuing from a principle of divine life. "Thy mercies are new every morning" is an utterance which on prophetic lips covers a very wide field. There was a belief common amongst the Jewish rabbis, that each night when the body sinks into repose the soul is taken out of it and washed by the Creator from the sins of the past day. Some such thought as this breathes in that sense of renewal which the child of Israel feels in contemplating each rising sun. He feels that he has awakened with more freshness than was present to him when he lay down, and he explains the increase in vitality by the newness of God's mercy every day. In the field of Christian thought men still hold this form of the ancient faith. The work which they look for from the Divine Spirit is emphatically a work whose mercies must be new every morning. When Paul says, "Though the outward man perish, yet the inward man is renewed day by day," he gives utterance to the self-same thought. He perceives that in the spiritual world there is a continuous need for the repair of tissue, and he knows that the tissues of spiritual life can only be repaired by the Power which first created them. Accordingly, his view of the Spirit's work is really the view of a perpetual creation—a creation in which the yesterday is ever being replaced by the to-morrow, and in which the vanishing products of the past are continually supplied by renewals of divine life.

Now, in the natural world no one can deny that the same principle is also a possible alternative. If we concede the truth of the alleged proposition that the organism experiences an increase of life in passing from the child to the man, we shall have no option but to conclude that what the Christian sees in the world of grace the scientist beholds in the world of nature. We have seen that the change from the child to the man cannot be effected by matter alone; and therefore, whatever that change be, we are bound to look elsewhere for the completion of its cause. If that change be an actual augmentation of life, and if matter has been found inadequate to produce such an augmentation, we shall be driven in the interest of science to a doctrine analogous to that which was held by the psalmist of Israel—the belief that the increase of life results from the impartation of a fresh vital stream.

Shall we, then, definitely adopt this view? Shall we say that the increase of life which marks the difference between the man and the child owes its origin to a direct intervention of the primal source of nature? We would certainly say so if we were convinced that that which marks the difference between the man and the child *is* an increase of life. But this leads us back naturally to the first of the assumed propositions, and the one to explain which the other two were formulated. The whole syllogism has been constructed by the scientist with the view of accounting for the alleged fact that there is more life in the man than in the child. What if this be not a fact at all? What if the explanation has been given to account for something which exists only in the theory of the observer? Is there really more life in the man than in the child? Let it be remembered that when we speak of life here we mean consciousness. None has ever denied that the transition from childhood to maturity is marked by an increase in the power of the physical forces, an increase which is amply explained by the assimilation on the part of the organism of the influences of material nature. But when we speak of life we always mean something distinct from these. Whatever our theory of life may be, whatever our view of its origin, whatever our sense of its destiny, we are bound in the interest of science to look at it as it actually manifests itself, and the form in which it actually manifests itself is consciousness. Other agencies may accompany it, other influences may condition it, other phenomena may flow from it, but the thing itself, as we know it, is consciousness and consciousness alone. When, therefore, we ask whether there be more life in the man than in the child, we must be understood to ask whether the man has more consciousness than the child. Now, for our part, paradoxical as it may seem, we are convinced that the man has not. We believe that there is not more consciousness, but, what is a very different thing, a consciousness of more. The eye which is circumscribed by a range of buildings is in a very different position from the eye which is permitted to travel freely over the expanse of wood and field; yet no one would assert that the difference consists in the fact of the latter having more sight. What it has in reality is more to see. The change is a change of environment, and the widening of the environment has simply brought into conscious action that power which already is latently present. Now the human eye is a mode of consciousness, and it is consistent with analogy to infer that what happens in one of its modes is the law for consciousness as a whole. We do not ask for the evolution of life the admission of any principle which is not equally recognised in the evolution of matter. It is strenuously maintained by every evolutionist that since the day of first formation there never has been any increase of matter in the universe. Nor is the evolutionist appalled by the fact that there is no resemblance whatever between the universe as it now appears and the universe as it must have been in the day of its first formation; he amply accounts for that fact by the difference of environment which material forms have in the interval undergone. We claim no more for life. Why should not consciousness be allowed to exist in the child in the same way that the powers now exhibited by matter are allowed to have existed in the universe? In the fire-cloud of primitive matter there was discernible only one power—gravitation; yet the result has shown that other powers were latent there. In the consciousness of the individual child there is manifested at the beginning only one feeling—the sense of pain. Why should not the subsequent result be allowed here also, to show that other feelings were latent there? The child has not less feeling than the man; it would be more correct to say that it feels *less*—*i.e.*, has a smaller number of objects over which its consciousness can range. The difference between the child's sense of pain and the man's sense of beauty is not a difference of quantity but of object. In respect of quantity the child in its agony of suffering may have a larger amount of sensation than the man in his perception of beauty. There is more than this; the comparison of the sense of beauty with any single feeling of individual pain is not a just comparison. When the child burns its hand, it has really only one sensation; when a man admires a landscape, he is successively experiencing a *variety* of sensations. We say successively, for no man can really experience two sensations at precisely the same moment. The true point of comparison, therefore, would be between the child's sense of pain and any one of those various sensations which make up the perception of beauty. Looked at from this standpoint, we shall probably reconsider our opinion that the man has more consciousness than the child. We shall probably come to the conclusion that the richness and variedness which distinguish the former from the latter are the result, not of an increased vitality, nor of a quantitively enlarged consciousness, but simply of those new modifications which the primitive life has undergone through its passage into other scenes.

We have now examined the three propositions of that syllogism which is the stronghold of scientific materialism. We have found that every one of them requires itself to be scientifically proved, and that to doubt the truth of any of them would not at present make us at variance with modern science. To have reached this conclusion is only, in other words, to say that the aphorism of the psalmist remains uncontradicted still. We do not forget that the materialist has another and an opposite door by which he claims to reach his inference. If he has failed to establish the theory that matter can *increase* life, he may still fall back upon the position that matter can diminish or annihilate life. He may still tell us that a blow on the head may deprive a man of consciousness. He will ask us, in the old spirit, whether the consciousness of the man after the blow is not less in quantity than the consciousness of the man before the blow; and if so, what could have made it less but the blow itself—in other words, the concussion of a material force. We must point out that this latter stronghold of materialism has nothing to do with the speculations of modern science. It cannot be ranked amongst the difficulties which the doctrine of evolution has thrown in the way of the old belief, for it existed long before the advent of the doctrine of evolution. Its origin as an argument does not lie with the man of science at all, but with the heart of man at all times in contemplating the old

old story, death. There is no mind, however superficial, that has not had its moments of perplexity in considering the apparent power of material influences to diminish the vitality of bygone years. It is not death itself which perplexes; that is an unknown quantity, and does not of necessity suggest any more than that the principle of life is away. That which casts a cloud over the mind is the process of dying, and the seeming decline of vital power which this process involves. That a mere form of physical disturbance should diminish consciousness, or should go to the extent of rendering a man unconscious, is from the spiritual side a very hard problem. From the spiritual side it would be an insoluble problem if we were bound to accept the apparent fact as real. But is it real? Do the data at our command lead inevitably to the conclusion that the disturbance in the physical framework has diminished the amount of consciousness? My perception of objects through a mirror is an act of consciousness. There are two conceivable ways in which that act may be arrested; you may cause me to close my eyes, or you may throw a covering over the mirror. Now, what happens in one particular mode of consciousness finds its precise analogy with consciousness as a whole. The process of dying interrupts the communication between subject and object, interposes a barrier to the mind's perception; that is the only fact within our observation, and beyond this all is inference.

The question is, What shall we infer? Shall we say that the eye of the mind is closed, or shall we say that a covering has been thrown over the mirror? The former is the view of the materialist, the latter of the spiritualist. The question is not, which of these views is most favourable to religion, most conducive to morality, most elevating to feeling? on all these sides it will probably be universally conceded that the spiritualist retains possession of the field. But the only point we are now concerned with is, Is the view of the spiritualist an anachronism in *science?* And it must be answered that on this subject the science of the nineteenth century is in possession of no fact which has not for ages been familiar to the most unlettered peasant. In the process of dying, what is that which the unlettered peasant sees? Simply an interrupted communication. He perceives the eye of his brother unable to respond to his eye, the ear unable to listen to his words, the hand unable to answer to his touch; he is convinced beyond all question that the intelligence which once communed with his own has now become oblivious to the sense of his presence. What, then, does the unlettered peasant conclude? Does he say that because his brother man is no longer conscious of *him*, the consciousness of that man no longer exists? No, he does not say so; and why? Because, peasant as he is, he knows as a matter of experience that there are innumerable cases in which the same unconsciousness of his own presence exists in union with the most vivid consciousness on the part of the very man who does not know him. He has heard the lips of his brother muttering in dreams, and expressing intelligence within the sphere of dreamland. He has had experience of the effect of fevers in which the patient, unconscious of all around, has yet betrayed by unmistakable signs that he is living all the time in a world of his own. With such facts in his mind, the peasant hesitates to draw the conclusion that the inability to communicate with himself is a proof of suspended consciousness.

Now these facts in the mind of the peasant are all the facts of the case. In other directions the man of science has an advantage over him; here they stand on an equal level. Before the mystery of the process of death, the distance between the simple and the learned is annulled, and science has to confess that it has no more authority than ignorance. In this region we are bound still to feel that we stand, as it were, at the opening of primitive life. We are in no higher intellectual position than we were at the dawn of human civilisation, have no more right to speculate, no more authority to dogmatise. The question then is, What shall be our attitude to the speculations of the past? We may say they are unproved, but by what line of reasoning shall we maintain that they are anachronisms?

Nearly three thousand years ago the Jewish prayer-book employed these words, "With Thee is the fountain of life." At the time when the words were written, all the facts of the case were known as familiarly as they are now; death was in existence, and death is the mystery of the seeming domination of mind by matter. The men who first chanted these words were thoroughly aware of the mystery of death, strongly impressed with its solemnity, and deeply alive to its horror. The fact which pressed upon them was precisely that fact which presses upon the scientist of to-day—the paradox of a seemingly immaterial element appearing to succumb to the force of material influences. Yet they never for a moment relinquished the belief that this element was immaterial, that it had its fountain in God. They have not left it doubtful why it was that the process of death did not shake this confidence. "I laid me down and slept; I awaked; for the Lord sustained me," are the words in which the psalmist expresses the ground of his confidence in life's perpetuity. He declares that in the light of the great miracle of sleep he will not be afraid of ten thousands of foes. His confidence lies in the fact not only that last night God awakened him *out of* sleep, but that He was sustaining him *in* sleep; he was only awakened because he had been all along *sustained*. To all outward appearance the vital element had been obliterated by the force of material influences, yet all the time it had been continuously preserved. It had been preserved because its fountain had never been matter, and therefore it was incapable of being diminished by the decay of its environment; its fountain was God, and therefore its duration was eternal. That was the reasoning of the psalmist based upon the most familiar fact of human experience, a fact which the advances of modern science have neither explained nor explained away. The scientist has the same difficulty as the psalmist, neither less nor more; he has the same solution as the psalmist, neither increased nor diminished in the force of its argument. He has no facts at his command on this question which were not equally at the command of the ancient Israelite, nor any suggestion to offer which seems more probable than that arrived at by the Jewish prayer-book; to him, therefore, it is not yet an anachronism to say, "With Thee is the fountain of life."

CHAPTER V.

THE PSALMIST'S VIEW OF HUMAN INSIGNIFICANCE.

Psalm viii. 3-5.

There is no subject which has been more fruitful in the hands of scientific scepticism than the change which has been effected on man's estimate of himself by the influences of modern culture. There is no writer who has dwelt more persistently on this side of the question than Mr Draper.[1] He labours to show how the intellectual development of Europe has tended steadily to contract the range of that vision which man has had of his own possibilities. The men of old time are compassionated and commiserated on account of their faith. It was not surprising, we are told, that those who believed themselves to be the astronomic centre of the universe should persuade themselves that all things in heaven and earth existed purely with a view to their welfare. It was not surprising that in the

[1] See his 'Conflict of Science and Religion,' chap. vi. and sequel.

insignificant estimate they formed of the magnitude of the visible universe their own little world should have assumed proportions extravagant and overwhelming. The times of this ignorance must be winked at, and we should be charitable to the weaknesses of our ancestors. But now, all men are commanded to repent. The time has come when a new heaven and a new earth have chased away the primitive darkness. The Ptolemaic system of astronomy is dead, and Copernicus reigns in its room. Man is no longer at liberty to think of himself as the centre of the universe; he and the earth on which he dwells are but insignificant atoms in a space which is fathomless, measureless. Modern culture has taught him true humility. The men of old time were children in knowledge, and therefore they had the pride of children; the man of civilised Europe has awakened to the vastness of the mystery that surrounds him, and has therefore the humility that belongs to a man. Those who believed that all other worlds revolved round this little globe of ours, might well speak of the counsels of heaven as devised for the good of man; but in the light of an astronomy which reveals this globe as but one of myriad specks in an infinite sky, the notion of such a human teleology becomes a delusion and a dream.

Such is the spirit of Mr Draper's reasoning. Yet nothing can be more certain than that, in one respect at least, he himself is subject to a delusion. Whether the light of modern astronomy does or does not furnish an argument for human nothingness, is a question which meantime may be left in abeyance. But whatever be the decision of that question, it is quite certain that the sense of human nothingness did not begin with the light of modern astronomy. It is too bad of Mr Draper to assume that the men of the past were ignorant of their insignificant position, when compared to the vastness of material nature. From any materialistic standpoint of comparison, the men of Israel at least were willing to acknowledge their inferiority not only to the vastness of the universe, but to things which Mr Draper himself would admit to be their subordinates. We have seen in a previous chapter how, from a materialistic point of view, the psalmist contrasts his own position unfavourably with that of the beast of the field, how he is not afraid to admit that the sparrow has found a house, and the swallow a nest for herself, while yet the spirit of man has received no adequate dwelling-place. And if on that occasion we found the psalmist recognising an inferiority even to the lower creatures, we are now to find him recognising a natural littleness in comparison with the celestial firmament. "When I consider Thy heavens, the work of Thy fingers, the moon and the stars, which Thou hast ordained; what is man, that Thou art mindful of him? and the son of man, that Thou visitest him?" How strangely modern the words sound! Leaving out the form of invocation, we could have imagined that there was speaking a *savant* of the nineteenth century. We feel that here is a man whom Mr Draper has no right to patronise, a man who is thoroughly awake to the vastness of that system in which he lives, and perfectly, painfully conscious how little right by nature he has to live there at all. He goes out beneath the stars and meditates at eventide, and his meditations are such as Mr Draper himself might have envied. Without knowing the Copernican system of astronomy, he reaches at a bound that conclusion which the Copernican system of astronomy is said to have attained. He arrives at the conviction that, measured by any natural standard, his own life has no glory in comparison with an all-excelling glory. He feels himself to be dwarfed by the magnificence and the variety of other worlds. He sinks into a sense of insignificance in the presence of a splendour before which his own light grows dim, and he expresses that sense of insignificance in language which Mr Draper himself would not deem unscientific, "What is man, that Thou art mindful of him?"

In one respect, indeed, the position of the psalmist is radically different from the position of Mr Draper. Mr Draper's wonder at the immensity of stellar spaces leads him to a spirit of scepticism as to the destiny of man. The psalmist's wonder, on the other hand, originates in the fact that he has already surmounted all scepticism as to man's destiny. It is not with him a problem whether God will or will not be mindful of man; he speaks after conviction that God has already been mindful. He does not say, When I consider the heavens, how can I believe that my little life has been an object of special interest to the Source of universal life? What he says is this: When I consider the heavens, and how insignificant I am from a materialistic point of view, I marvel at that divine condescension which has manifestly made such provision for my wants, which has set all things on earth under my feet, and crowned me with the glory and honour of being king over this present world.

And truly, no one can say that this wonder of the psalmist rests on an unscientific basis. God, evolution, nature, the creative principle, called by what name you will, has not only done great things for man, but has done as great things for man as for any other object in the universe; every evolutionist in the world will admit this. So great is the evidence for a teleological plan in human nature, that if its existence be denied in human nature, it must be denied everywhere. The basis of the psalmist's wonder, therefore, is the only scientific basis. We must start from the undoubted fact that man is conscious in himself of a marvellous adaptation to his wants in the system of nature, conscious of a harmony between his desires and the objects which fulfil them, of a congruity between his faculties and the world on which they are exercised. To admit this fact, and no one has ever denied it, is really to recognise the truth that the interests of man have been cared for by some power in the universe. Whether we call that power God or evolution, whether we term it conscious or unconscious, is not here the question. Man is what he is by reason of that system of nature in which he dwells. This being so, it is surely legitimate, even on scientific principles, to wonder at that confluence of circumstances which have conspired to make him what he has become, and to inquire, in a spirit of scientific and religious reverence, what has been the origin of that which looks so like a mindfulness of man.

Mr Draper, indeed, would object very much to the word "mindfulness"; it would suggest to him that very notion of teleology which he regards as a relic of barbarism. He would be willing to allow that man has become what he is through the evolutionary convergence of circumstances, but he would altogether reject the doctrine that this evolutionary convergence has been the result of intelligent foresight. The unpardonable sin of the psalmist would, in his eyes, be just his reference of these circumstances to an intelligent foresight. To say that God is mindful of man is to make man an end in the universe. What age but one of primitive ignorance, especially of astronomic ignorance, could ever have conceived such a thought? If the Jewish nation had known the Copernican system, would it have been possible for it to have fallen into such folly? It believed man to be the centre because it believed the earth to be the centre, and its belief that the earth was the centre was the product of its ignorance of the vastness of the material system.

Such is substantially the view of Mr Draper, and the view of that whole class of writers who have seen, in the scientific development of the nineteenth century, a ground for pitying the ignorance of the past. Now there is no doubt whatever that, in the days of the Israelitish psalmist, men did believe the earth to be the centre of the universe, and there is equally little doubt that in this belief they were wrong. But the whole question here is, What effect had this primitive belief on the primitive religion of mankind? Mr Draper thinks that the primitive belief in the mindfulness of a Supreme Being was caused by the notion that the earth was the centre of the universe. To us, on the other hand, it is perfectly clear that, so far as Israel is concerned, the order of procedure was exactly the reverse. Instead of the Psalmist's conviction of God's mindfulness being caused by his belief in the earth's centrality, his belief in the earth's centrality was caused by his conviction of God's mindfulness.

To him the first object of contemplation was God Himself. We in modern times are in the habit of seeking God in the light of all things; the psalmist seeks all things in the light of God. To him God is before all things, and His will is the sole ground of their being. If he believes man to be endowed with glory and honour, it is not because he thinks that there is anything in the nature of man which is worthy of this glory and honour, nor anything in his astronomical position which has helped to make him dignified. It is because he believes that God's sovereign will has chosen man. He recognises human dignity as the simple result of divine election, and everything that seems to favour that dignity as a provision of the same election. He thinks of the earth as the centre of the universe, simply because God has chosen to make it so; this is really the thought which lies at the back of the words, "The earth is the Lord's, and the fulness thereof." And the fulness of the earth to him is man; the material is chosen for the sake of the immaterial. So far from seeing in man a being who is favoured on account of the earth's centrality, he sees in the earth's centrality a result of that elective favour which, in the good pleasure of the Eternal, has been bestowed upon the human race. The psalmist, in short, is, like all the men of his nation, an anticipative Calvinist; he lives in the thought of God, and outside the thought of God he cannot admit the life of anything. It is vain, therefore, to ascribe the teleology of the Hebrew to his ignorance of the earth's astronomic position. He *was* ignorant of the earth's astronomic position; but this was an effect, not a cause. If we want to prefer a charge of ignorance against the Hebrew on the ground of his teleological views, we must prefer that charge against the teleology itself. We must not say that he was incompetent to speak of the great Source of nature by reason of his inadequate view of astronomy; it was not astronomy that led him to his notion of God. The greatness of stars and systems was to him not to be measured by the vastness of their dimensions and the extent of their distances; their greatness lay in the fact that they were manifestations of the life of God, that they declared His glory and showed forth His handiwork. The question is, Was his notion of God Himself erroneous? Did his primitive ignorance appear in the conception he formed of the Deity as well as in the conception he formed of the stars? When he said that God was mindful of man, when he declared that the human was an object of solicitude to the divine, did he state something which science has proved an anachronism? That is the question, and the only question with which we are here concerned. It is not simply between the scientist and the psalmist; it is between the scientist and the religious sentiment at its root. On the answer to it depends the solution of the problem whether religion shall or shall not continue to exist. If there be no capacity for mindfulness in God—in other words, if God be not a Being of whom we can predicate the attribute of thought—there is no use of pursuing the subject any further; let us say at once that the age of science is the antithesis of the age of religion. But if the conception of scientific evolution is not in itself opposed to the presence of a mind in nature; if the order of natural law, as expounded by modern physics, is not proved to be incompatible with the order of an intelligence working behind the law,— would it not be scientific to pause before charging with primitive ignorance a nation whose sole offence has been the recognition of a God who is mindful of man?

Let us ask, then, if Mr Draper himself has rightly diagnosed the facts of the case. He holds that the belief in evolution must for ever destroy man's sense of his own dignity, by denying him that central position in the astronomic universe which in primitive days he was wont to claim. Is it the fact that the doctrine of evolution does deny to man a central place in the astronomic or in any other universe? Paradoxical as it may seem, and contrary to the common statement as it certainly is we contend that the doctrine of evolution does no such thing. What the doctrine of evolution does deny is that man can any longer be regarded as the centre of the universe, exclusively or peculiarly. It does not take away his central position, but it insists that this central position shall be shared by everything else in turn. There are two ways in which I may deny that London is any longer to be regarded as the capital of the British empire. I may insist that for the future the metropolitan dignity shall be transferred to Dublin, or I may enact that henceforth the metropolitan dignity shall every month be assigned to a different city of the empire until each shall have enjoyed the privilege of centrality. Now, if evolution had taken away the centrality of the earth in the former sense, there would have been great ground for Mr Draper's scepticism. If it had said that henceforth the central position was to be given to Jupiter, or Mercury, or Venus, there would have been very good ground for asking, not in a spirit of gratitude, but of incredulity, "What is man, that Thou art mindful of him?" But when evolution denies the centrality of the earth it is only in the latter sense. It will not allow the earth any longer to hold its central position as a monopoly, as a privilege unshared by other things. But in asking the earth to give up its central position as a *monopoly*, evolution does not ask it to give up its central position in itself. It only insists that the earth shall henceforth recognise the fact that it is not the sole or exclusive centre; that the privilege which it enjoys is a privilege which every object in the universe equally enjoys, and to which every object in the universe can equally vindicate its claim.

What *is* the doctrine of evolution? It is the belief that every part exists for the sake of the whole, and that the whole exists for the sake of every part. Let us observe the latter half of this definition; it is the one which is most frequently overlooked. That every part exists for the sake of the whole—in other words, that the whole would not be what it is if any one of its individual parts had been modified in its structure—is a truth which will be grasped by all minds scientific and unscientific. But it is not at first sight so clearly seen that the whole equally exists for the sake of every part; indeed, for any clear insight into this truth we are indebted to the doctrine of evolution itself. When an event happens in a humble village, we are accustomed in philosophic moments to say that it will produce influences beyond itself, will indirectly affect the whole structure of society. To say so is both philosophic and scientific, for it is a fact of observation that the whole structure of society is bound by a single chain. But it does not often occur to us, even in philosophic moments, to say that the humble event here specified has been the end towards which all other events have been converging, that it owes its very existence to the combined operations of the united universe. Yet that is the doctrine of evolution. The lifting of a feather by the wind is the result of the entire process of nature which went before it. If we had knowledge perfect enough we could trace back to the very beginning of nature the process by which the feather was lifted, and we should find that, trivial as the act appears, it yet owed its being to the entire course of the preceding order of things. Now, let us imagine for a moment that this feather were to be gifted with an intelligence sufficient to comprehend its own position in the universe. What, in such circumstances, would be its opinion of itself? Would it not be very much the same as that opinion which the psalmist formed of the human nature within him? It would feel, on the one hand, that it was marvellously small and wondrously insignificant in comparison with the objects around it, quite unworthy in itself to occupy any place in the temple of nature. And yet side by side with this feeling—nay, growing directly out of this feeling—there would be a strong surprise at the fact that it actually did occupy not only a place, but the central place in this natural temple. For this intelligent feather would recognise that it was indeed the centre of the universe; it would say, as the psalmist said of himself, What am I, that nature is mindful of me? for it has put all things under my feet. It would find what the psalmist found—that its life had been an end in the universe, and an end towards which the universe itself had been working. Nor, on the principles of evolution, would the discovery in any sense be a delusion. It is the direct doctrine of evolution that everything is what it is just through the co-operation of all other things; in other words, that any single object waking up into scientific intelligence would be justified in beholding itself as the centre of the universe. It could write a history of the universe with the express purpose of showing that all things had been making towards itself, and its purpose would be vindicated by actual scientific proof; it would be able without difficulty to demonstrate that, alike in its genesis and in its exodus, the stream of universal being had been working towards the consummation of its own individual life.

Now, instead of the hypothetical feather let us take the actual man. He has, as a matter of fact, come into existence in a way unknown to himself. His deepest conviction is not that of natural dignity, but that of natural weakness. He is impressed with his nothingness and insignificance amid the forces of material nature, and in a large number of cases it is this sense of nothingness which has been the parent of his religious worship. Nevertheless, what happened to the hypothetical feather happens to the actual man, and for precisely the same reason. In point of fact he is the only creature on the earth who has been gifted with a scientific intelligence—in other words, the only creature who has received a vision of that central position which he shares with every other creature, and which every other creature would claim if it had only the same vision. He writes the history of creation with a reference to himself as the centre; he tells how the herb of the field was made for his use, and how the beast of the field was made for his service. In doing so he is in full accord with the principle of evolution, which declares him to be indeed the centre. It is true the principle of evolution equally declares that the herb and the beast of the field are also centres. But then neither the herb nor the beast of the field is endowed with that scientific intelligence which can make it conscious of its centrality. Man alone has this possession, and therefore man alone has written the record of the convergence of all things towards his own being. Accordingly, it is not unscientific in the psalmist to wonder at the prominence of one naturally so insignificant, to say to the Power who represents his ideal of culminated nature, "What is man, that Thou art mindful of him?" He only says what in other language every evolutionist might say in contemplating how any single object results from the united whole. The truth is, Mr Draper is under a delusion in supposing that the doctrine of evolution has contributed to divorce the thought of the psalmist from modern sympathies. Its effect, on the contrary, has been of rather a reactionary nature, has tended somewhat to bring back the old conception. There was a time in which men were indeed prone to ask in a spirit of scepticism, "What is man, that Thou art mindful of him?"—it was precisely at that epoch in which the former skies were passing away and new heavens were breaking upon a new earth. The age in which Copernicus proclaimed that the system of Ptolemy was no longer tenable, was the age when man felt the psalmist's sense of insignificance without the psalmist's wonder at the manner in which the insignificance had been compensated. He felt that he could no longer regard himself as the special centre of the visible universe, and he was driven back into the position of one who stood infinitely remote from all influences of protective care. This was undoubtedly the tendency of the age immediately succeeding the Reformation. But where Mr Draper goes wrong is in making an age of transition the characteristic period of all scientific development. The Copernican system of astronomy was a preparation for the doctrine of evolution, but it was not itself the doctrine of evolution, and when that doctrine came it destroyed its negative aspect. Evolution has taken away that very sense of distance which the first discovery of the Copernican system created between man and the universe. It has served as a bridge over that seeming gulf of infinitude which the first discovery of the larger dimension of the heavens left before the eyes of men. The infinitude of the universe still remains, but it is no longer an infinite void; it is a universe permeated by a chain whose first link is intimately connected with its last, and whose every part is necessary to the production of the whole. Man has lost his position as the *exclusive* centre of universal nature, but he has regained that position in combination with all other things. No object, however minute, is in the light of this new doctrine too insignificant to be a centre; no event, however trivial, too unimportant to have its place in the development of the mighty whole. The doctrine of the correlation of forces has revealed the wondrous truth that the same power which plays on the surface operates also at the interior, and that the force which acts at the extremities of the universe is identical with that force which lies at the centre of all being.

We arrive, then, at this conclusion: The psalmist of Israel was not guilty of primitive ignorance in feeling himself to be the centre of the universe. He was as alive as Mr Draper to the natural insignificance of man, and was prompted to utter his words by the very sense of that insignificance. He felt that by nature he had no right even to be, much less any claim to aspire to the height of being. It was this feeling of insignificance which awakened his surprise, a surprise originating in the fact that this puny life of his was yet something whose influence ramified into all other things, and which in turn all other things conspired to influence. This was the paradox which was awakened in the heart of the psalmist—the paradox of the mingled littleness and greatness of man. And that conclusion has not become an anachronism; it is as true and as paradoxical to-day as it was in the days of ancient Israel. Man is still conscious of his utter impotence amid the forces of material nature, and he is made every day increasingly conscious that these forces have a relation to his impotent life. The paradox of the psalmist remains the paradox of the evolutionist, and the latter must ask his Universe as the former asked his God, "What is man, that Thou art mindful of him?"

CHAPTER VI.

THE PSALMIST'S TWOFOLD CREATION.

PSALM xix.

In the previous chapter we found the psalmist engaged in contrasting the condition of man with the condition of physical nature. On that occasion he had not yet risen above the view of man as a physical being; he had contemplated him only as one of the many forces which operated throughout the universe. Viewed from this physical standpoint, the psalmist had been naturally impressed above all other things with the insignificance of man amid the forces of material nature, and his main wonder had been that, in spite of his insignificance, he had yet obtained amongst these forces a central and a commanding position.

But in this nineteenth psalm to which we now turn, the psalmist has altered his standpoint. He has come to see that the reason of man's pre-eminence over the forces of material nature is the possession by man of a force which is not material. The creation, which at first presented itself to his eye merely as a physical unity, is now seen breaking up into two parts, the one physical and the other moral. Viewed as a mere physical entity, man had been simply a part of nature, and a very insignificant part indeed. But now there rises in the view of the psalmist a region in which man is no longer a part of physical nature, and in which his position cannot be measured by anything that is material. This psalm, in short, is the revelation of a dualism in a sphere which was once perceived only as a unity. The world of creation divides itself before the eye of the psalmist into two distinct worlds,—the one material, the other moral—the one comprehending the physical firmament, the other embracing the statutes of the heart. The German philosopher Kant has said that there were two things which uniformly filled him with wonder—the starry heavens above, and the moral law within. The psalmist is impressed with the same twofold wonder —the marvel of the heavens that declare the glory of God, and the marvel of those moral intuitions which rejoice the heart and make the simple wise.

Now, let us observe at the outset that in the view of the psalmist these are not two creations, but simply two aspects of the same creation. They are indeed contrasted aspects; the psalmist is quite unable to find in either of them any connecting link by which it could pass over into the other. But that connecting link which he fails to find *in* them, he discovers *behind* them. The marvel of the starry heavens is not to be explained by the marvel of the moral law, nor is the moral law to be accounted for as an evolution of the starry heavens. Nevertheless these two worlds, distinct in themselves, are united in the fact that they come from a common source; the glory which the heavens declare is the glory of God, the perfection which the moral law displays is the perfection of "the law of the Lord." Now we must recognise the fact that, notwithstanding the great distance in time and the great transformation in form of thought which have intervened between the days of the psalmist and our own, the conclusion here arrived at is no anachronism; it is in strict accordance with the latest results of science. The latest result of science is the doctrine of evolution, and the doctrine of evolution is simply the effort to find for all things a common source and a united origin. It does not yet profess to tell the precise steps by which any one form of existence developed into another; what it does profess to hold is that all forms of existence, however diverse they now may be, were originally derived from one parentage and took their start from a common home. What that parentage is, science does not say; it confesses its inability to give it a definite name. Sometimes it calls it the Unknowable, sometimes Force, sometimes Power, sometimes the Order of Nature, but in each case it prints the word with a capital letter, to express the conviction that its meaning transcends description. Now the psalmist of Israel agrees with the modern scientist in the belief that all forms, however various, may be traced to a single source. He differs from the modern scientist in giving that source a definite name; he calls it God. But this difference is in no sense a contradiction. The modern scientist will not affirm that the common origin of all things was a personal life, but as little will he deny it. To affirm it, therefore, cannot be unscientific; it can at most be only beyond science. It is one thing to say that faith belongs to a region which science has not yet traversed; it is another and a very different thing to say that the region traversed by faith is at variance with the region traversed by science. In pronouncing the ultimate source of things to be indefinable by name and unknowable by nature, science has left a marginal sphere open to the flight of faith. The psalmist has occupied that sphere; he has ventured to define that which science has left undefined. He has given a name to the ultimate source of all things; he has called it God. We may not say that in so doing he has followed the lines of science; it may be that the lines of science do not yet stretch so far. But we can say without the slightest fear of contradiction, and by the admission of science herself, that the psalmist's definition, however much it may transcend, does not interrupt her lines. There remains the additional fact that on one great point they are already in unison. The latest results of scientific research have come to the same conclusion arrived at by the primitive religious sentiment— that the sources of creation are not many but one, that all variety had its original home in unity, and that the manifold divergences which divide the worlds of matter and spirit may be traced at last to a common centre.

The next thing we have to observe in the psalmist's view of creation is the order in which he arranges its objects. He confines his attention to the two objects which Kant signalises as the things which fill him with greatest wonder — the starry heavens and the spirit of man. The first part of his hymn of praise is devoted to the starry heavens; the last part to the human spirit. Why does he put the heavens first, and the spirit of man last? Not because he considers the latter to be inferior to the former, for he distinctly and expressly states the contrary; admitting that the heavens declare God's glory, he maintains that the moral law contains God's perfection. Why, then, does he place last in order that which he emphatically holds to be first in quality? Clearly because the order he is following is not one of quality, but of time. He places the heavens first because, in his view, they came first in the order of creation; he places the spirit of man last because he regarded the spirit of man as the latest manifestation of the glory of God.

Now the point for us to observe is this, that the psalmist has here unconsciously described that very order of creation which is followed by the modern evolutionist. The first step of the evolutionist is the unfolding of that process by which the heavens came to declare the glory of the universe. A nebulous fire-cloud is made the parent of all things animate and inanimate. Every product of nature, human, animal, vegetable, and mineral, is ultimately traced back to the existence of this celestial fire, which, at the beginning of time, at once comprehended and concealed all other existences. The glory of the heavens, therefore, is, in the view of the modern evolutionist, the nucleus of every other glory, the original centre out of which radiated those varied streams of light and life whose manifoldness now delights the eye. And if, in the view of the modern evolutionist, the glory of the heavens was the earliest product of the great process of development, the latest product of that process has been the spirit of man. Alike by the verdict of the evolutionist as by the verdict of the psalmist, the spirit of man has entered upon the scene only towards the end of the day, and that law of human morality which the psalmist declares to be the perfection of the divine glory, has come into being simply as the last result of that process of development which the formation of the heavens began.

Having now looked at the psalmist's view of creation as a whole, let us proceed briefly to consider that creation in the twofold aspect in which it presented itself to his eye. We begin with its outward or visible manifestation, that which occupies the earlier part of this psalm, and which we found in the eighth psalm awakening him to a sense of personal insignificance. There is, however, a difference between the attitude which he occupied toward the starry firmament on the former occasion, and the attitude which he occupies here. In Ps. viii., as we have seen, the heavens created within him a sense of depression; they made him feel small. In Ps. xix., there is no trace of such a feeling; he contemplates the firmament of worlds with an eye of unqualified delight, a delight which springs from the fact that he is not dwarfed in the contemplation. In the former psalm, the aspect of nature for a moment made him feel the depression of the Brahman; here he is able to view it with the exultation of the Greek. On the former occasion, the heavens had only declared the glory of God; here the glory of God had become his glory too.

Can we find in the contents of these psalms anything which will justify this change of standpoint? It seems to us that we can. In Ps. viii., the psalmist was only considering a work which had been completed; in Ps. xix., he is contemplating a work which is still being transacted. The God of Ps. viii. has already "*set* His glory," and man is only called to contemplate the result of ages that are past; the effect of such a contemplation is inevitably to make God distant from the soul. But the God of Ps. xix. is even now in the act of manifesting His glory; the heavens are declaring it, the firmament is showing it; the psalmist feels himself to be in the very presence of the God of creation, and privileged to be a spectator of His creative process. This appears evidently from the words, "Day unto day uttereth speech, and night unto night showeth knowledge." The reference, as we think, is to the first chapter of Genesis, in which each separate act of creation is ushered in between the evening and the morning. Here, in the view of the psalmist, the evenings and the mornings of Genesis are no longer merely historical moments in which, ages ago, the divine glory once manifested itself; they are the symbols of constantly recurring periods in which the divine glory is ever manifesting itself. The evening and the morning still enclose the creative acts of God; day utters speech unto day, and night teaches knowledge unto night. Nor is the process to the psalmist less impressive because there is no longer a record of the audible voice of God. God is not heard saying, "Let there be light," "Let there be a firmament," "Let the dry land appear." "There is no speech and there is no language," says the psalmist, the divine voice is not heard; none the less is there the evidence of a silent eloquence, "Their line is gone out through all the earth, and their words to the end of the world."

Now, in this vivid delineation of nature the psalmist is again in unconscious sympathy with the spirit of all true science, pre-eminently in sympathy with the spirit of evolution. The doctrine of modern evolution is the belief in a force or energy which is acting *now*. It does not hold, it does not admit that the energy of nature has been for a moment suspended, or that the original force which animated creation has been one tittle abated. It is true, the modern evolutionist hesitates to affirm that the process is still going on by which at first one species was transmuted into another. Even men of so advanced a type as Sir John Lubbock believe that the gulf between the animal and the man is now impassable; and so uncompromising an evolutionist as Mr Fiske is not afraid to affirm that, in his opinion, man marks the climax of the process of development. But while modern science is not disposed to expect a repetition of the first *effects* of evolution, it does not for a moment admit that there has been any suspension of its *powers*. The powers may never be combined in the same way, but they are none the less there, and none the less active. Every moment of consciousness is, in the view of modern science, a moment of evolution. The world is a series of transformations, in which the one Force is perpetually changing its form, and presenting endless aspects of multiplicity and variety. The life of the universe, which is really the life of one continuous day, is broken up by the partition of its one Force, into a succession of mornings and evenings, in which day unto day utters speech, and night unto night showeth knowledge. Creation here, too, has ceased to be viewed as a merely historical incident; it has become the manifestation of universal history itself. The Power which presides at the centre of things is no longer a power which merely sits and superintends; it is a force which pervades and animates the mighty whole. So far, the spirit of modern science is in strictest harmony with the spirit of the ancient religious sentiment, which is only in other words to say that the ancient religious sentiment has proved itself independent of time, and vindicated its claim to be the ever-fresh life of the Eternal. The modern scientist, when he deifies Nature, is really deifying a present in opposition to a past God, is asserting his belief that the Power which rules the universe is a Power which even now is immanent *in* the universe. The psalmist of Israel had precisely the same thought in view when he lifted his voice to God in the hymn of creation. He desired to see the work of creation not simply as a work which was begun, continued, and ended long ago, but as a process which at that very hour was passing before his sight, and as a miracle which at that very moment was raising his heart to the contemplation of the Father's glory.

But there is yet another aspect of this outward creation as it presented itself to the eye of the psalmist—an aspect which perhaps cannot be better described than by the word *continuity*. The God whom he worships in nature is not merely a God who is immanently present in all His works; He is a God who makes each of His works link on to one another, who connects the parts together until they form a united whole. This, we think, is really the thought which most prominently underlies the words, "Day unto day uttereth speech, and night unto night showeth knowledge." Recognising in the spirit of the Book of Genesis the division of the created universe into different compartments, he yet recognises between each of these compartments a fixed bond of connection. There is a creative work for to-day, and a creative work for to-morrow, but the creative work of to-day has a *reference* to the creative work of to-morrow; the periods are joined together so as to form a unity: "Day unto day uttereth speech, and night unto night showeth knowledge." When the psalmist says of the starry firmament that its line has gone out unto all the earth, and its words unto the end of the world, he is expressing, in almost scientific language, his sense of the unity of creation; he is expressing his belief in the fact that, between all the works of God, from the least to the greatest, there is an indissoluble cord of union which makes the welfare of the one indispensable to the welfare of the other. The starry firmament is the earliest manifestation of creative power, yet the starry firmament, although the first, has a determinate influence upon the latest product of creation; its line and words, although seemingly above all contact with the world below, have yet gone forth to the very end of that world, and influenced the last stages of its development.

It is to bring out this thought that he makes reference to the position of the sun, whose tabernacle is in the midst of the starry heavens, and which cometh out of his chamber as a bridegroom rejoicing. The joy consists in the fact that, although his tabernacle is above, the race which he runs reaches to the extremities of the universe; that his going forth is to the end of the world, and that there is "nothing hid from the heat thereof." Now, scientifically speaking, this language in our day would not be considered accurate. The sun is not the circumference of the universe; his going forth is not to the end of the world; strictly speaking, he does not go forth at all. And yet the thought which the psalmist designs to convey is completely unaffected by such changes in scientific conception. The doctrine of evolution really aims, in other words, to establish the self-same position—the position that all things move towards a common unity, that day utters speech unto day. The modern source of unity is no longer specially the sun, but it *may be* the sun, or any other object on which we shall choose to fix our attention. In the view of the evolutionist every object is in turn the tabernacle in the midst of the firmament, for every object can be proved to have been what it is simply by the convergence towards it of all other things and circumstances. So, too, though in a literal sense the sun no longer makes its circuit unto the end of the world, the principle of the psalmist's description remains scientifically true. In modern times we estimate the extent of an object's movement by the extent of that impact which it produces on other things. The sun keeps within its settled tabernacle, but from the recesses of that tabernacle it radiates forth influences of which it is no exaggeration to say that their going forth is unto the end of the world. We use the word "world" here as the psalmist used it — in its widest, most comprehensive sense, including both the earth and the heavens. The sun, as we now know it, is only the ruler of the solar system; yet, on the principle of evolution, it influences every system of the universe. The heat which it generates is not an isolated phenomenon, but a phenomenon which modifies the existing condition of the universe at large, so that with the psalmist we can literally say that there is nothing hid from it. The only difference between the psalmist's conception and ours is that, in our scientific view, the same thing may be affirmed of every object which, for the time being, we may consider apart. We must not forget, indeed, that in the view of the psalmist there was really an invisible bond of unity behind all—the Power whom he called God. But even here science in its most materialistic form will not gainsay his principle. God to the psalmist was what the universal whole is to the scientist. He, like the scientist, beheld the evidence of an invisible cord binding together the fleeting images of sense. This was to him the equivalent of that permanent Force which the evolutionist declares to be incapable of either increase or diminution; he could say of its immutability, amidst the perishableness of its own fleeting manifestations,—"They shall perish, but Thou shalt endure; yea, all of them shall wax old like a garment: as a vesture shalt Thou change them, and they shall be changed, but Thou art the same."

It will not be imagined that in these remarks our design has been to show that the psalmist of Israel had any glimmering anticipation of the modern doctrine of evolution. He had no such anticipation. Evolution was a thought not so much opposed to him as simply foreign to him; it had not entered into his mind, and therefore it had never become to him an object of comparison with other theories. The one thought of the psalmist was that the universe owed its perpetual creation to the presence and the breath of the Eternal, that its life was every moment of every hour sustained by His life. Into the mode of that sustenance he did not care to inquire; such knowledge was too high for him, and he did not attempt to understand it. He contented himself with the fact, and the fact to him was clear; the heavens declared God's glory, and the firmament showed forth His handiwork. But what we wish to show is this, that the same view may be held consistently with our modern theories of nature. We have desired to prove that the religious sentiment of the psalmist has not been rendered an anachronism by any discoveries of the scientist, and that in the process of transition from the old heavens into the new there has been carried over the basis for the construction of a faith in God.

We have now completed our survey of that part of this psalm which refers to the outward creation—the declaration of God's glory in the starry firmament. We come next to the consideration of that glory which in the view of the psalmist has been set above the heavens—that law of the Lord which is written in the heart of man. With this second glory he deals in the concluding half of the psalm, and he strikes the key-note at the very outset by declaring that notwithstanding the grandeur of the starry firmament it pales before the majesty of the moral law, "The law of the Lord is perfect, converting the soul." Let it be observed on what ground the psalmist gives the preference to God's moral over his physical law. It is not on the ground that the physical law exhibits any defect in its construction or any inability to fulfil its own decrees; in this respect the psalmist would have been the first to admit that the physical law has the seeming advantage over the moral. He saw clearly that the stars of the firmament fulfilled their march without a step out of tune, while the lives of individual men were perpetually in discord with the divine decree. But what to the psalmist made the moral law superior, was the fact that it *did* deal with man. The law which regulated the stars of the firmament was equally perfect in itself with the law which regulated the destiny of human lives; they were both the one law of God applied in two different ways. But while the law of the firmament was equal in perfection to the law of the soul, the firmament itself was not equal to the soul. The firmament was something mechanical which could be dealt with on merely mechanical principles, something which was capable of being moulded from without and incapable of resisting from within. But the soul was of an altogether different order. It was impossible to say to it by a mere mechanical mandate, "Let there be light"; to have brought forth its light in this way would have been to make it a star and not a soul. It was something possessed of will, and therefore it could not be influenced by mechanism; it could only be approached from within. It differed from all other parts of the creation in this, that it was capable of resisting the divine decree, that in point of fact it had resisted it. Unlike the stars of the firmament it had broken away from its orbit, "and found no end, in wandering mazes lost." The first work of divine power had to be exerted in bringing it back, in converting it. And the psalmist felt that this conversion of the soul required a greater exercise of power than the direction of the heavens, simply from the fact that it was a soul. The heavens were naturally plastic; like the clay of the potter they had no power to say, Why hast thou made us thus? But the very idea of a human will was the idea of something which had a choice of its own, and whose choice might possibly be in an opposite direction to the orbit selected by the heavenly Father. The choice made by the human will had in point of fact been in this opposite direction; the soul was moving in an orbit diverse from the circle of the Infinite perfection. It was necessary before all things that it should be turned round, "converted," and the turning round of a soul was a vastly more delicate operation than the turning round of a world. To turn a star of the firmament from one course into another would simply be to change its mode of action, but to turn a soul from one course into another is to change its mode of thinking; the evil lies primarily in its thought, in its choice, in its will.

Accordingly, the conversion of the soul is made by the psalmist the grandest manifestation of the power of God, the act which exhibits the very perfection of His glory. And to him there is significance in the fact that the most perfect manifestation is the latest. We have seen that in order of time he places the starry firmament first among the manifestations of divine glory, and sees in the perfection of the moral law the latest of all its products. In this he is in strict accordance with that conception of the writer of Genesis, with which he is probably familiar. In the view of the writer of Genesis the order of creation is an order upwards, an order in which the second is better than the first and the last highest of all. That is not first which is spiritual, but that which is natural; afterward that which is spiritual. The ascent of the creative development is an ascent from the formless to the formed, from the void to the coherent, from the Spirit moving on the face of the indistinguishable deep to the Spirit distinctively animating a human soul. Here, as in the case of the psalmist, we have a double law, or rather a double manifestation of one and the same law. The first glory of God is a glory in the heavens, and it shines forth in obedience to the divine command, "Let there be light." The last glory is the glory in the heart of man, and here the law of the Lord is perfect. It is perfect because it no longer manifests itself through an object which springs into existence by the mere command to be, but because it exhibits itself in the very image of the Divine, in the action of an intelligent will and the movement of a conscious heart. The final stage of manifestation is the highest stage of glory, "The law of the Lord is perfect, converting the soul."

CHAPTER VII.

THE PSALMIST'S GROUND OF RELIGIOUS CONFIDENCE.

Psalm cxxxix.

IN the previous chapter we considered whether the religious sentiment has been affected by the transition from the old into the new conception of nature. We have now to consider whether the religious sentiment has been affected by the transition from the old into the new conception of man. For it must be remembered that the change from ancient into modern thought has been a change that has extended not only to the natural but to the human. There was a time when man was regarded as something unique in the order of creation. All things had their birth from God, but man was born from God in a very special way, in the manner of an only-begotten. His entrance into life could only be accomplished by a miracle, a leap, a paroxysm, in which the old was in a moment transcended by something radically and wholly new. Now this is not the conception which modern science has formed of the nature of man. In the light of the evolutionist he can no longer be regarded as a leap or paroxysm in the order of the universe. The universe has no leaps or paroxysms; all its parts are linked by an iron chain. Man, therefore, in this conception has no right any longer to look upon himself as distinctive; he is bound to view himself as a part of nature, and to take his humble place as one of the many rivets which connect the universal chain.

Now it is no part of our province here to say whether the modern scientific conception of man has or has not been proved. We are not in any sense discussing the merits or demerits of the doctrine of evolution; our whole aim is to consider whether the doctrine of evolution would, if established, demand a modification or an extinction of that ancient religious sentiment which we have found represented by the psalmist of Israel. We must therefore, for the sake of the argument, assume that the modern conception of man is the true and established conception, and must try from this basis to see whether the religious sentiment is in any danger of becoming an anachronism. Now at first sight it would seem as if the change from the ancient into the modern conception of man involved nothing less than a destruction of the religious sentiment. As long as man was looked upon as something distinct in the order of creation, he might naturally and reasonably be supposed to have a special claim to divine knowledge; made in the image of God, it could not be denied that he had a right to know God. But when it is held that man, instead of having a distinctive place in the order of nature, is at best only the flower and crown of nature herself, the case is altogether changed. If the human soul is generically one with the life of all other things, what right has it to claim a privilege peculiar to itself? what right has it to attribute to its own imaginings a source more supernatural than those influences of nature which produce the bloom of the flower? It is the answer to this question which has given rise to that modern spirit which has permeated the ranks of science and influenced the teachings of philosophy —the spirit of agnosticism. Agnosticism claims to be the direct result and the immediate corollary of the doctrine of evolution. There was a time when men aspired to know God, and took the name of Gnostics in support of that claim. Their conclusion was a legitimate inference from their premiss. They held that the spirit of man was an emanation from the Spirit of God, and therefore they were logically right in affirming that the human spirit could know the divine. But evolution has disproved the distinctive greatness of man, and thereby it has denied that there is anything within him which is specially divine. It has claimed to find his origin in union with the origin of all other things, and thereby it has refused to recognise in him a transcendental source of knowledge. The conclusion which was logical in the gnostic has become impossible to the evolutionist. The gnostic saw the human spirit descending from the Spirit of the Highest, and it was only natural that in the aspirations of the human spirit he should read the thoughts of the Highest. The evolutionist sees the human spirit ascending from the lowest forms of life, if not of matter, and it is only natural that, conceding the truth of his premiss, he should read in the aspirations of man but the latest flowerings of a material germ-cell.

Now the question is, What would the psalmist of Israel say to this if he were to be transplanted into the heart of our age? The question what one of the ancients would think in beholding the aspects of modern life is commonly a very absurd one, for there is generally no standard of comparison by which modern life can put itself into even a momentary sympathy with ancient culture. But our contention is, that in the present instance there *is* such a standard of comparison. We are trying to prove that there is one thing which has survived entire amid the transition from the old into the new, and that is the religious sentiment. As the highest representative of that sentiment in ancient times, we have taken the psalmist of Israel. We wish to inquire how the religious sentiment of the psalmist would be affected by the speculations of modern science, and therefore it is no absurd supposition to imagine him for a moment in contact with these speculations. We ask, then, what would be his impression if he were permitted to stand a while in the presence of our modern culture? We do not ask whether he would accept that culture as an ultimate standard of truth; assuming that he did accept it, we wish to know what would be his view of his own previous religious sentiment. Happily we have at our disposal the means of answering this question. We have placed at the head of this chapter the reference to a psalm whose conclusions are more far-reaching than the psalmist himself contemplated, and whose truth, if admitted for any age, must be allowed to have a universal application. Let us turn, therefore, to its utterances, and see whether they can still be read in the light of modern times; whether the faith which they imply is a faith which can continue to endure in the face of that doctrine of evolution which professes to make all things new.

The evolutionist, as we have seen, tells us that we can no longer admit the spirit of man to be a distinctively separate creation; that, on the contrary, we must in the last analysis regard it as the flowering of that primitive germ-cell in which all life began. The psalmist of Israel would not for a moment have been staggered by such an assertion as this, even had he admitted it to have been demonstrated. He would not even have been staggered by the step in advance made by some evolutionists who tell us that the human spirit is the flowering not only of a primitive germ-cell, but ultimately of primitive matter. We have proof from this psalm itself, as we shall see in the sequel, that the psalmist of Israel would not have felt himself one iota lowered by this discovery. He would have said: You tell me that the spirit of man is only the latest bloom of a piece of matter; what of that? the piece of matter itself is a thought of the Absolute Spirit. You cannot rob me of my descent from God by telling me that I have come from darkness; the darkness is itself a portion of His light. If, as we believe, the writer of this psalm belongs to the Persian period, his words acquire a very deep significance. We know that the doctrine of Parsism was a doctrine which denied the common origin of the universe from one divine Source. It admitted the existence of a principle of light, and from that principle of light it believed that all bright things came. But it beheld also dark things in the world, and it had to account for their existence too. It could not account for them by an origin from the principle of light, and therefore it supposed an opposite origin. It postulated the being of a principle of darkness, an element whose action in the world was antagonistic to the movement of the power which it called light. If we read the psalm in this view, we shall receive a wondrous amount of suggestiveness from its words and phrases. Look, for example, at the bold expressions of verses 11 and 12: "If I say, Surely the darkness shall cover me; even the night shall be light about me. Yea, the darkness hideth not from Thee; but the night shineth as the day: the darkness and the light are both alike to Thee." The psalmist is quite willing to admit that in the movement of the universe there is a principle of reaction as well as action, that there is something which holds back as well as something which forwards the progress of mankind. He is quite willing to admit that so far as the present world is concerned, there are some things whose origin must be referred not to the advancing but to the retarding element. But then the psalmist goes on to say that the retarding element is itself a portion of the infinite light. He cannot believe that any principle in the universe whatever is ultimately apart from God. However unlike to the divine nature it may now seem, however reactionary to the line of human progress it may now be, he feels convinced that originally it had its place in the plan of development, and was itself a product of the will which said, "Let there be light."

Now the application to modern science is more direct than it might at first sight appear. In the view of the Parsee, the principle of darkness in the universe was matter; it was this which weighed down the spirit and became the origin of sin and death. When, therefore, the psalmist said that darkness could not cover from God, he probably meant to say that materialism could not shut out from the necessity of God, that the dark shade which men called dead matter was itself a form of infinite light and life. It is impossible to avoid the conclusion that this, or some thought analogous to this, was in the mind of the psalmist of Israel when he said, "Whither can I *flee* from Thy presence?" The question with him was not where God could be found, but where God could not be found. His objection to the doctrine of the Parsee was that it undervalued too much the objects which it called things of darkness. We can find no clearer illustration of this than the bold reference contained in the words, "If I make my bed in the place of the dead, Thou art there." If there was one thing which to the Jew was associated with the absence of God, if there was one thing which to the Parsee was linked with the thought of the principle of darkness, it was the place of the dead. To the natural view of each of them it was the opposite of light, a sphere from which the Divine Presence had for ever fled away. And yet the Jewish prayer-book transcends the natural consciousness of the nation. At so early a stage as the date of the twenty-third Psalm, we find an inspired singer proclaiming, "Though I walk through the valley of the shadow of death, I will fear no evil: for Thou art with me;" and here, perhaps in the very heart of Persian influences, we are confronted by an utterance bolder still, "If I make my bed in the place of the dead, Thou art there." Now the application of this to modern scientific theories is not difficult to see. If the psalmist was willing to find the presence of God even in the place of the dead, if he was willing to recognise even in the disintegration of matter a form of the divine life, he would certainly not have been startled by the doctrine that the genealogy of earthly things could be traced back to something material; he would have said in the same spirit, If I go back to dead matter, Thou art there.

And if we look deeper we shall see that in the psalm before us there is almost a direct statement of this very point. Read the striking words of verses 15 and 16: "My substance was not hid from Thee, when I was made in secret, and curiously wrought in the lowest parts of the earth. Thine eyes did see my substance, yet being unperfect; and in Thy book all my members were written, which in continuance were fashioned, when as yet there was none of them." One would almost imagine the psalmist had been living in the nineteenth century, and had uttered the words as a direct answer to the theory of Mr Darwin. In what sense the psalmist understood his own words it is now impossible to say. It seems to us very likely that he was in intellectual contact with some prevalent theory regarding the origin of man. Perhaps some Persian *savant* had laboured to show that the earthly or material part of man's nature had an origin in common with all other things, that the element which he called his natural life was identical with those physical forces which played over the face of nature, and that this physical life itself had been slowly and progressively developed by the successive acts of that nature. Such theories as these were as common in ancient philosophy as they have become in modern times, and if the writer of this psalm lived in the Persian period he would breathe the very atmosphere of them. What, then, is his answer to such a view of man's nature? It is practically the answer which is given by the writer of the Book of Genesis when he places the human soul at the last stage of creation, and looks upon it as for that very reason the first thing in the thought of God. The psalmist declares himself willing to accept the doctrine that the creation of man was a development. He declares himself willing to believe that the substance of his being was not constituted in a moment, but that at first it was imperfect. He declares himself ready to admit that the members of his body did not spring up contemporaneously, but were fashioned continuously and in a graduated scale of sequence. But then he goes on to tell why it is that he is able to bear such a thought with equanimity. It is because already in the germ he sees the bloom of the flower, because already in the imperfect substance he beholds the completed human soul. Nay, however slow may be the process of development by which the imperfect substance passes into the human soul, he regards the act of creation as completed even in the germ,—"In Thy book all my members were written, when as yet there was none of them." He looks upon God's creative act as first spiritual and then natural. As spiritual it is a thought, and as a thought it already comprehends the whole. The members as they appear in time may be fashioned one after another, but as they exist in eternity they are seen in their full complement. The idea is evidently that of an earthly artist. The work of the earthly artist progresses slowly in its manual labour; its members are fashioned continuously. But in the mind of the artist himself the picture is finished from the beginning. If it were not finished from the beginning, the work of continuous fashioning would be less perfectly executed; it is the glory of the completed ideal which guides the hand in the performance of the outward labour. This is the thought which the psalmist imputes to the divine art of creation. Its latest stage is man, and it is a stage which historically is only reached by slow gradations. But that which is last in history is first in artistic conception. Man may have arisen from an imperfect substance, and his members may have been fashioned by slow degrees; but in the thought of the Divine

Artist he existed before the imperfect substance, and in the book of the divine conception all his members were simultaneously written.

Now no man can say that such a view is an anachronism; the most that can be said is that it is incapable of scientific proof. It is a thought which in itself is perfectly compatible with the most advanced form of the doctrine of evolution, and would have been accepted by the psalmist in the face of such advancement. We do not forget, indeed, that certain attempts have been made to prove such a conception of nature to be incompatible with science. Mr G. H. Lewes has treated this teleological view with much contempt, and has striven to show that it is contradicted by the facts of embryology. The doctrine of the psalmist is the doctrine of a divine plan which sees an end at the beginning, and works towards that end through all its stages. The world exists for the sake of man, and every step in the making of the world is really a step in the making of man. Now what Mr Lewes says is in effect this: Would any architect, whose design was to make a palace, begin by drawing the plan for the construction of a hut, and afterwards proceed to draw another plan for the construction of a cottage? If we saw him act in this way, would it not be reasonable to conclude that he had no design of making a palace, and that in attributing to him that design we were mistaken? Yet this is precisely the state of matters which embryology discloses in the actual development of nature. The human fœtus does not all at once become human, but passes successively through the gradations of fish, reptile, bird, and mammal. If the being of man is the result of a design contemplated beforehand by a Divine Artist, why does not that Artist proceed at once to the goal? If he designs to construct a man, why does he begin by constructing successively a fish, a reptile, and a bird? And seeing this is notoriously the course of nature —seeing the order of arrangement is actually the reaching of a palace through successive attempts to construct huts and cottages—is not the reasonable inference here also that we have been mistaken in attributing the origin of the human soul to a primordial design in the plan of a Divine Artist?

Such is the reasoning of Mr G. H. Lewes based upon the facts of embryology. Whether these are yet ascertained facts may perhaps be doubted, but they are for the most part accepted by the modern evolutionist, and therefore for the sake of the argument they must be accepted here. The question then is, Has Mr Lewes made out his case against the existence of a teleological plan in nature? He asks if an architect who designed to erect a palace would begin by constructing successively a hut and a cottage. We answer, No, provided the palace had nothing to do with the hut and the cottage. But what if this was designed to be a palace which was to include within its interior a number of other structures, the hut and the cottage amongst them? In this case, would not the preliminary construction of these inferior and subordinate structures be one of the direct steps to the achievement of the ultimate goal? And if in looking at the completed palace we found that its interior contained such subordinate structures as huts and cottages, would we not be justified in attributing the previous construction of these to the existence of a primordial plan which from the beginning had fashioned the whole? Now we submit that in the instance actually in question these are the facts of the case. Man has been called a microcosm of the world, and he has been called so with truth. He is that palace which contains within itself a multitude of huts and cottages. In addition to that nature which is distinctively his own, he has within him the nature of those things which his life has transcended. He encloses the life of the plant and the life of the animal, the principle of spontaneous growth and the principle of instinctive desire. Exalted as his humanity is above these, they are yet instrumental to the life of his humanity; they are no longer the rulers of his nature, but they have become its ministering spirits. And if the possession of these lower structures is seen to be an advantage to the palace of the human soul, how can the facts of embryology be supposed to be adverse to the argument of final cause? How could man have within him the spontaneous growth of the plant and the instinctive desire of the animal, unless at some period of his history the life of the plant and of the animal had formed a portion of his own life? And at what period of his history could such a participation be more natural than in that stage of embryonic formation in which the human temple was building? Was it not fitting that the palace which was to include the inferior structures should, in the process of its construction, begin by making trial of those structures? If the remains of an animal nature are recognised as advantageous to human development, if the instinctive impulses of an earlier creation have their use in the moral life of man, could a Divine Intelligence have more signally manifested its presence than by causing the life of man to incorporate in the hour of its formation the developments of a former day?

To return to the view of the psalmist. We have seen that the ground of his religious confidence did not lie in any theory concerning the distinctive dignity of man, did not consist in any belief that the human race was distinguished from other races by an origin from above. The ground of the psalmist's confidence was rather the assuming of a contrary position. He delighted to think of man as having had a common origin with all other things; only, he considered that origin to be not dead matter, but a living God. He was not frightened by the notion that it might be possible to trace a line of connection between man and matter, but what prevented him from being frightened was his sure and steadfast belief that matter itself had its origin in the life of the Eternal. The conviction of the Divine Omnipresence, the belief that there was no spot where God could not be found, the certainty that neither the imperfections of primitive substance nor the disintegrations of dead matter could really shut out the influence of some form of the divine life, was the power which lifted the heart of the psalmist above every gathering shadow, and sustained him from every temptation to follow the seen and temporal.

It may be said, indeed, that all this leaves untouched the difficulties raised by the modern doctrine of agnosticism. If the life of man be not immediately derived from the life of God, if it comes from God only as all other things come from Him, what value is he entitled to attach to his own meditations on the divine? Is not the religious sentiment of the psalmist based upon an exactly contrary position, and therefore on a position at variance with modern science? Does not the ground of his confidence consist in this, that, being immediately derived from the life of God, he has a right to know God?

Now we shall not here inquire as to the psalmist's view of mediate or immediate derivation. We are disposed to think that a Jew would have been incapable of recognising any distinction between them. He would not have regarded a life as coming less directly from God because it had to pass through several intermediate stages before reaching its completion. He would not have admitted that these intermediate stages were in any sense second causes; he recognised the existence of no second causes, and therefore whatever proceeded from God at all, must, in his view, have proceeded from God immediately. But, waiving this question, what we want to remark is this, that the consciousness of personal knowledge was in no sense the ground of the psalmist's confidence. No modern agnostic could have expressed himself more strongly than he does in the very words of the psalm: "Such knowledge is too wonderful for me; it is high, I cannot attain unto it." We are in a great mistake in imagining that the reason of the Jew for being a theist was his belief in the infallibility of his own knowledge. The truth is, he was, more than the man of any other nation, impressed with the impossibility of anything entitled to be called a knowledge of God; the key-note of his teaching was this: "Canst thou by searching find out God? canst thou find out the Almighty unto perfection?" The second commandment of the Decalogue is based upon the doctrine that the essential nature of the divine is incapable of being represented by the human. It is forbidden to make any image after the likeness of things in the heavens, or on the earth, or in the waters under the earth; because it is intended to impress upon the soul that no object in the sky, or on the plain, or in the sea, could for a moment depict the essence of the divine nature. The Jew, in fact, so far from being, as is often supposed, the votary of a sensuous worship, is of all worshippers the most inward and the most spiritual; his reverence is the product of his humility, and his humility is the result of his sense of intellectual ignorance.

What, then, is the ground of his religious confidence? It is not, as we have seen, his knowledge of God; is there any other source from which it can flow? Yes; there is another source,—God's knowledge of *him*. And if we examine the sacred records of Judaism, we shall find that this is the true source of the national confidence in God. In this very psalm, which we have taken as a representative of the Jewish religious consciousness, we find that almost designedly a line of distinction is drawn between man's knowledge of God and God's knowledge of man. On the one hand, as we have seen, the psalmist is not afraid to express his sense of the inadequacy of man's intellect to grasp the things that are eternal; he speaks in language which agnosticism itself would employ: "Such knowledge is too wonderful for me; it is high, I cannot attain unto it." But on the other hand, when all this is said, there is a ground of religious consciousness which to him remains untouched; he cannot know God, but God can know him. It is God's knowledge of him that constitutes the real source of his hope: "O Lord, Thou hast searched me, and known me. Thou knowest my down-sitting and mine uprising, Thou understandest my thought afar off." He is not concerned with the question whether his thought represents adequately the nature of God; the fact that comforts him is the conviction that his thought, however inadequate it may be, is itself the work of God, an emanation of that Divine Presence which besets him behind and before. The whole circle of time is to him filled with God. The past is behind him, but it is not dead; it lives in the life of God, it is beset by God. The future is before him, but it is not contingent; it is already a part of that Divine Presence which sees the end in the beginning. The present is with him, and its difficulties press upon him, but its pressure is recognised as itself the weight of a Divine Hand, a burden laid upon him by the very contact of his soul with God. This is the ground of the psalmist's confidence. It is not that he is able by an act of intellectual intuition or by a process of natural reasoning to scale the heights of heaven and unveil the presence of the Eternal; it is rather that the presence of the Eternal is every moment manifesting itself in the very veil of time, and comprehending the life of man in the very things which man cannot comprehend.

It will be seen how near, from one point of view, this conception of the psalmist approaches to the religious attitude of Mr Herbert Spencer. We say, from one point of view. Mr Spencer is not a theist —that is to say, he refuses to take the name of theist, or to call the power of the universe by any name. He would therefore demur to saying, "Thou hast known me." He would equally demur, however, to saying, "Thou hast *not* known me." He does not hold that the ascription of omniscience to God is forbidden by anything in science; to say that it is so forbidden he would consider to be itself unscientific. He insists upon the Power which we recognise in the universe being recognised by us as an undefined power. Accepting provisionally, therefore, this qualification, there yet remain points in which his conception is strongly analogous to the conception of the psalmist. He calls his God by the name of the Unknowable, by which he means to express the fact that no searching can find Him out; the psalmist, too, has expressed the same fact in the candid admission which he makes in the very heart of his theism, that the knowledge of God is too wonderful for him, so high that he cannot attain unto it. But while Mr Spencer holds that no man can by searching find out the inscrutable

Force which presides at the centre of the universe, he holds not less strongly and tenaciously that the Force at the centre of the universe is the life of all other forces and the source of all other things. Itself uncomprehended, there is yet nothing which is not comprehended in it; itself incapable of being found, there is nothing which does not find its being in it alone. There is no difference between great and small, there is no contrast between high and low; the atom and the world alike are the manifestation of the stupendous Power whose distinctive feature is just the fact of its omnipresence. Mr Spencer would have echoed to the full that sentiment of the psalmist which has included in one comprehensive unity all the works of nature from the least unto the greatest. No one can read this 139th Psalm without being impressed with the manner in which the most trivial and the most gigantic objects are alike comprehended as manifestations of the Divine Omnipresence. We are not surprised to hear the writer say that if he ascends up into heaven he will find God there; but it seems a curious conjunction to place side by side with such a range of divine majesty the comparatively insignificant power of being able to search his own finite soul, of being able to comprehend such trifling things as his rising up and his sitting down. It would be a curious conjunction to any but a Jew and a modern scientist; but to the Jew and the modern scientist it is of all things the most natural. To the Jew everything lived in the life of God, and in the life of God alone; he could say with uncompromising consistency, "Whom have I in heaven but Thee? and there is none upon earth that I desire besides Thee." To the modern scientist also, as represented in the person of Mr Herbert Spencer, there is a primal and underlying Force which constitutes the life of all. So much does it constitute the universal life, that it dwarfs all distinctions between individual things. It ascends up into the heavens, and it extends to the place of the dead; it compasses our path and our lying down, and it reaches to the uttermost parts of the sea. Nay, strange as it may seem, there is a sense in which Mr Spencer applies to his primal Force the same counteracting tendency to an evolutionary materialism which the psalmist finds in it; he too can say, "My substance was not hid from Thee, when I was made in secret, and curiously wrought in the lowest parts of the earth." It is his aim to show that morality is an evolution, and that what we now call the dictates of conscience were once the maxims of utility. But after having completed his survey of the evolutionary process, Mr Spencer goes on to tell us that the instincts of conscience have not thereby lost their value, for they must ultimately be regarded as the manifestations of that primal Force whose being is inscrutable and whose action is persistent. Here, in the age of the most developed culture, have we not found a regress to the argument of the psalmist? Has not science in the very heart of her stronghold admitted that the faith of ancient Israel was in its essence no anachronism, and that, after the process of evolution has been traced back to its lowest substance, this substance itself vindicates the divine origin of the world by revealing in its construction the presence of a higher Power?

CHAPTER VIII.

THE PSALMIST'S OPTIMISM.

PSALM cvii. 1-9.

THERE is one peculiarity about the scientific speculations of the nineteenth century which cannot fail to arrest the attention of an observer; it is the fact that in spite of the apparent dreariness of the conclusions to which they seem to point, the men who conduct them have a hopeful view of the universe. One would imagine, *a priori*, that a doctrine which professed to level all things into a common origin, would proportionately see all things on a common level, would entertain very moderate notions of the future possibilities of man. Yet strange as it may seem, the tendency of evolutionary science has been, on the whole, an optimistic tendency. If on the one hand it has been ready to say of man's origin, "What is man, that Thou art mindful of him?" it has on the other hand been equally ready to say of his destiny, "It doth not yet appear what we shall be." The theory of Darwin may entertain very low ideas of the source from which humanity has sprung, but it for the most part cherishes a very high estimate of the goal to which humanity is going. Whether, with Mr Fiske, the evolutionist regards man as the ultimate stage of the development of nature, or whether, with others, he prefers to look upon him as but preparatory to a higher stage of being, man is in either case contemplated as in possession of a lofty destiny. Even Professor Clifford, who of all modern scientists has shown least sympathy with the religious spirit, has not scrupled to reveal his hope that the course of evolution itself will ultimately unlock a new sense in the human organism, and usher the human spirit into the glory of a new revelation. By a widely different method has he not here arrived at the very conclusion of Christianity when it bids us hope for the advent of a day in which we shall see no longer through a glass darkly, but behold with unveiled face the glory of the universe?

We have called this attitude of modern science an optimistic *tendency;* we have not given it the absolute name of optimism. The scientist does not believe that this is now the best of possible worlds. He is of all men most eager to insist on the frightful struggles which nature has to pass through before she can reach her goal. But the optimistic tendency of modern science appears in the belief that nature passes through these struggles *in order* to reach her goal. It is the distinct doctrine of evolution that whatever amount of perfection has been reached in the present, or will be reached in the future, must be regarded as the result of all the evolutionary steps which have preceded it, the struggles of nature included. This is a very important admission, an admission which very easily lends itself to the argument of the theist. It is not denied by the evolutionist that, as a matter of fact, the course of the world has been one of progress. Evolution, as Professor Huxley says, is consistent with standing still, or with regress, just as much as with progress; none the less is it true in point of fact, that in relation to our world progress has been the form which evolution has assumed. It is admitted by the modern scientist that the earth is now in a very different position from that which it occupied in primitive ages; to say so is simply to assert that the law of evolution, as we have it, is a law of upward development. Over against this advantageous state of matters we have to place the fact that in the course of this upward development there has been a sacrifice not only of myriad lives, but of myriad races; and this has often been used as an argument to counteract the proof of theism. But strange to say, the answer has come from the camp of evolution itself. The evolutionists are never weary of telling us that the world is what it is just by reason of every step which it has taken in the past; that if one single step had been taken differently, the whole aspect of present things would have been essentially different. Here, then, the argument which was supposed to be against theism, has, in the hands of its very supporters, become an argument in its favour. The world has admittedly reached a stage which, in comparison with previous stages, might be called perfection. We are told that it would not have reached this stage of comparative perfection if a single step of its course had been different from what it has been. Now, amongst the steps of its course must be ranked those very struggles for existence which many have supposed to be unfavourable to the doctrine of a divine benevolence, those numerous and multiform destructions of life which have marked the ladder of ascent towards the spirit of man. However sorrowful it may be to contemplate these, they can, in the light of the doctrine of evolution, no longer be regarded as obstacles to the belief in a divine benevolence. The doctrine of evolution declares that the stage of perfection at which we have now arrived, is the result of every step which has preceded it, and that any alteration in any of these steps would have nullified our present position. What is the inference? It is, that instead of maligning the order of nature on account of the many lives it has destroyed, we ought to see in the destruction of these lives an evidence of natural order. If our present perfection could not have been, had the past been otherwise than it has been, it follows inevitably and irresistibly that the apparent cruelties of nature have not been cruelties at all, but have been themselves steps of that ascending ladder on which life has climbed to the spirit of man.

Such is the logical conclusion from the modern doctrine of evolution. The view of nature to which it points is evidently an optimistic view. It is built upon the notion that in the present system of nature all things have worked together and are working together for good. It does not commit itself to the position that in a system of evolution all things *must* work together for good; it recognises in evolution possibilities of degradation as well as of elevation. But taking the system of nature as we find it, and estimating the world as it actually exists, it is not afraid to declare that whatever perfection we have now reached is the direct result of the stages of preceding imperfection, and would not have been achieved without the antecedence of these stages. Evolution, therefore, as it is manifested in the system of nature, not only presents no barrier to the acceptance of a divine benevolence, but actually clears away the barrier which was left standing by preceding systems. It claims the dark shades of the universe as preparations for its coming light, and appropriates the struggles and the deaths of countless generations as necessary steps to the attainment of that good which we have now achieved.

The question which now arises is this, What relation does this view of modern science bear to the intuitions of that primitive religious sentiment which is represented in the psalmist of Israel? We shall best arrive at the answer to this question by considering what relation the view of the psalmist of Israel bears to the views of surrounding and contemporaneous religions. The three great religions of the East contemporaneous with the faith of the psalmist were Confucianism, Brahmanism, and Parsism. Each of these will be found to embody a distinct view of the universe. Confucianism is a system of completed optimism. The Chinese empire is taken to represent the world, and the Chinese empire is believed to be a realisation of the kingdom of heaven. Confucianism is thus a recognition that the Messianic age has already come. Its world is the best possible world. The possibility of any change is not admitted, because any change could only be a decline from the existing perfection. China has refused to progress, simply from the fact that she does not admit any room for improvement; she has reached the belief in present optimism. Brahmanism is the extreme opposite; it is a system of pessimism. It regards the world as even now a non-existent thing—a dream, a delusion. It does not so much look upon it in the light of something tending towards degeneration as in the light of something which is now at the lowest. Brahmanism, in truth, recognises no development either upward or downward; in this respect it agrees with Confucianism. Confucianism denies the possibility of development, on the ground that there is no step higher; Brahmanism denies the possibility of development, on the ground that there is no step lower. Intermediate between these, yet distinctively different from either, is the system of Parsism. The Parsee is unable to see in this world either a vision of perfect happiness or a vision of perfect misery; he feels what men in everyday life feel, that there are times of light and that there are times of darkness. And, like many men in everyday life, he is quite unable to reconcile the times of darkness with the times of light. The difference between him and ordinary men is, that while the ordinary man simply grumbles, the Parsee makes a philosophy of his grumbling. Unable to reconcile the times of darkness and the times of light, he maintains that they are incapable of reconciliation, and that therefore they must have proceeded from opposite sources of being. He contends that there cannot be one single principle from which all things have come; there must be two principles, one good and the other evil. There must be a principle of light which shall account for the existence of the bright things of life, and there must be an element of darkness which shall explain the being of its dark things. It is true, the Parsee is ultimately an optimist, because he believes that the light will finally conquer the darkness. Nevertheless, in his view, the world as it now stands is a composite world, a double creation, the product of two unreconciled and irreconcilable forces; it is destined to be divine, but as yet it is half divine and half diabolical.

Now it will be observed that in all these systems there is a process of elimination; each of them has constructed itself only by mutilating or by destroying some other fact of the universe. Confucianism has laid hold of the prosperity that exists in the Chinese empire, and converted it into a universal element, ignoring altogether the fact that there are regions beyond China and that there are regions within China which are not prosperous. Brahmanism has laid its hand upon the truth that there is much misery in this world, and that much of what men call happiness proves to be delusion; but in declaring the world itself to be a delusion, it has closed its eyes to the other truth that there are lights as well as shadows, and that some lights are not illusory but real. Parsism has been less one-sided than either of them. It has freely admitted the existence both of lights and shadows, and has refused to see either an absolute good or an absolute evil. But while Parsism has admitted the *existence* of both, it has refused to recognise their coexistence;

it has insisted on seeing a great gulf fixed between them, so that the one by no possibility can come into contact with the other. Parsism, therefore, while apparently more impartial than the two preceding systems, has really mutilated more than either of them; it has eliminated the universe itself. That which makes the things amid which we live a universe, is simply the fact that they are referable to a single source; deny their common origin, and you deny them the name of a universe. Parsism admitted lights and admitted shadows, but the lights had nothing to do with the shadows, and the shadows had nothing to do with the lights. Parsism, therefore, mutilated more than all beside, because it eliminated that bond of union which makes it possible to regard this world, not as a floating panorama, but as an order of universal law.

Now, in striking contrast to all these systems stands that faith of Judaism which we have taken as representative of the religious sentiment. It is precisely by reason of its contrast in this respect that we *have* taken it to represent the religious sentiment. Even from the most naturalistic point of view, there is something almost if not altogether unique in the position of the Old Testament faith. It seems to us to be the only religion of primitive times which has erected itself into a system without either eliminating or mutilating any fact of the existing world. We have seen how Confucianism existed by ignoring the darkness, how Brahmanism lived by ignoring the light, how Parsism sustained itself by denying any possible connection between the darkness and the light. These forms of ancient thought are representative forms; they stand for the three tendencies between which the philosophies of the past have been uniformly divided. Confucianism, Brahmanism, and Parsism will be found to have been reproduced in the creeds of the Epicurean, of the Stoic, and of the Manichean—the one dwelling on life's brightness, the other on its darkness, and the third on the impossibility of finding a common origin for its darkness and its light. Now it is in contrast to these tendencies that the religion of the Old Testament stands out most conspicuously. Here for the first and last time in ancient history we have a faith which aspires to reconcile those elements of the universe which other faiths had pronounced irreconcilable. Here for the first and last time in the religious life of the past we are confronted by a religion which in the spirit of a later science seeks to present the universe as a united whole, and strives to refer to a common origin those materials of the world which contemporary nations had deemed mutually discordant. Recognising with Confucianism the element of joy which the world contains, accepting with Brahmanism the element of sorrow which life reveals, this religion has yet refused with either to exclude the other from its system. Nor is it content with Parsism to allow the joy and the sorrow of life to exist as antagonistic elements; it insists on finding for them a source in one common fountain. It has been sometimes affirmed that Judaism derived its conception of Satan from its captivity in the land of the Parsees; we shall not here dispute the point. Wheresoever it derived its conception of Satan, it made that conception unique and peculiarly its own. The Satan of Judaism is no longer identical with that principle of darkness which is acknowledged by the Parsee. He is in no sense a ruler of the universe; he has only a delegated power. The only ruler of the universe is the infinite Jehovah, and besides Him there is no other. Not only has He no rival, but He has no second; He is Himself the origin of all things. The Jew is not afraid to say, "Shall there be evil in a city, and the Lord hath not done it?" He cannot admit for a moment that the system of the universe is anything but divine, nor can he admit that, being divine, anything can be excluded from its range. Sorrow cannot be cast out into a realm of accident, chance, contingency. The wars that desolate the world, the rumours of war that disturb the souls of men, cannot be relegated to a sphere where some other principle reigns than God. All these seemingly adverse elements must be gathered within the fold of a Divine Providence. They must have their appearance of adversity destroyed by receiving a place within that comprehensive plan, where all things work together for good, and where God is all in all.

Judaism then is distinguished from other contemporaneous religions by its recognition of the universe as a united whole, by its power to set apart a place for the action of suffering in a system of divine goodness. It seems to us that there are recognisable two stages in the development of this thought of Judaism. In the first of these, the sufferings of life are regarded as punitive, as penalties divinely inflicted for the sins of the people. In the second, the sufferings of life are regarded as remedial, as that process of crucifixion whereby the sins of the past are not simply punished, but excised. The transition from the former to the latter is the Book of Job, marking at once the end of the old epoch and the beginning of the new. The first conception of suffering has become unsatisfactory. Men are waking up to the truth that the so-called penalties of life are by no means limited to those who most deserve them, and the patriarch of Uz is seen to protest against that belief, which until his days had been the orthodox one. He claims for the sorrows of life a yet higher place in the divine system than had hitherto been conceded to them. Hitherto they had been recognised as coming from God, but only in the form of penalties; Job asks for them a still closer approximation to the circle of the divine life. As yet, indeed, he is unable to see the positive good of suffering; he is actuated rather by faith than sight. The one thing which he does see, and see clearly, is that the idea of punishment alone is not adequate to explain the ills which flesh is heir to. He sees men of undoubted probity, when measured by any human standard, subjected to a train of calamities from which men of less probity are free. He beholds the godless sitting in gilded state and the godly oppressed with toil, and he asks if these things ought so to be. It is clear to him that, if the old theory be the true one, they ought not. If the sole design of the sorrows of life be to mark the divine anger against some act of transgression, it followed inevitably and conclusively that the men who had most of life's sorrow should be those who had committed most transgression. If the actual state of things was different from this, if the calamities of life were often more severely laid upon the good than upon the evil, it followed that there must be some other and some deeper explanation of that mysterious law of suffering which has made the whole creation subject to vanity.

Accordingly, the Book of Job marks the transition into another view of the universe, a view which makes the seemingly discordant elements still less discordant with the original plan of good. To say that suffering was designed as the penalty of sin was certainly to give it a place in the divine economy; it was at the very least a free admission of the truth that God is all in all. Yet the place here given to suffering was, after all, but an accidental place. It was something which existed in the universe merely because in the universe there was something which had gone wrong. It was no part of God's ideal, no portion of that divine plan which had said, "Let us make man in our image;" it was sent only because the divine plan had been frustrated and because the divine image had been broken. But in this second conception of suffering it was all the reverse. The place of sorrow in the world was no longer an accidental place. It was no longer something which resulted merely from an infraction of divine law; it was itself a part of the original law of God. According to this new conception the sorrows of life were themselves a portion of that divine ideal which had prompted the design, "Let us make man in our own image." The ideal there contemplated was the thought of a being who should be fit not only for Eden but for Gethsemane, who should be perfect not merely without suffering but through suffering, who should be like God not simply because he was innocent but because he had known the difference between good and evil and had chosen the good. In such an ideal of human glory, suffering was necessarily present from the beginning. Instead of being an accident, it belonged to the very essence of a pure humanity. Before man could enter into his glory he was bound to suffer, because that which was to make his glory was itself the experience of trial.

Now this is the thought which from beginning to end pervades that 107th Psalm which we have made the motto of this chapter. Like many other psalms it is an expression of thanksgiving for the goodness of God; but the goodness of God is here viewed in a very advanced light. In the earlier epoch of Jewish development, man's sense of God's goodness was limited to his experience of outward prosperity. Here the ground of thanksgiving is man's sense of the benefit which has been wrought on him by adversity. The men who are called to give thanks are, "The redeemed of the Lord"—*i.e.*, those who have been emancipated from a past slavery. But the idea throughout the psalm is, that the emancipation is more valuable than the original freedom, that the man is more free by reason of the antecedent slavery than he would have been had he never been enslaved. Accordingly, the thanksgiving is offered not for the redemption alone, but for that previous state of calamity which made the redemption necessary; the cross receives a distinctive place in the list of those divine benefits which man is not to forget. The whole thought is expressed metaphorically in verses 23 to 25, where we are exhorted to see the wonders of God in the deep, and to contemplate the elevating effect of the storms which sweep over the sea: "He commandeth, and raiseth the stormy wind, which lifteth up the waves thereof." The same idea is expressed without metaphor in verse 9: "He satisfieth the longing soul, and filleth the hungry soul with goodness." In these words the spirit of Judaism has almost touched the spirit of Christianity, altogether touched it so far as theory is concerned. Doubtless its ideal is as yet in advance of its power, and its thought of what ought to be outruns its capacity for practice. Yet the ideal itself is the ideal of Christianity. The psalmist has already reached that view of human suffering which appears so resplendently in the Sermon on the Mount, and where, in direct antithesis to the spirit of the earlier epoch, the element of human sorrow is declared to be an avenue to final joy. The psalmist of Israel is already in anticipation beholding that vision of beatitudes where the poor in spirit are seen exalted to the kingdom, not in spite of but by reason of that poverty, and where the sons of sorrow are comforted just on account of their mourning. He too has penetrated into the secret of a higher mission for the so-called ills of life than that of merely vindicating the majesty of an outraged and offended law, for he has arrived at a perception of the truth that a sense of spiritual want is the premonition of spiritual riches, and that the hunger of the inward life is the proof not of famine but of plenty.

Now we say that this conception of human suffering is more allied to the spirit of modern science than any other conception which the mind of man has yet entertained. At first sight it might seem as if this were a paradox. The doctrine that all things work together for good would appear on a superficial view to have little affinity with a system of evolution where the weakest go to the wall and the strongest alone survive. But this, as we have said, is only a superficial view of the system of evolution. It is true that in this system there are things which go to the wall and there are things which survive, but the things which survive only do so because the others have gone to the wall; it is really a case of life being perfected by death. The proof of this statement is, as we have seen, derived from no extraneous source, but from the direct testimony of the doctrine of evolution itself. That doctrine affirms that the world in its present state of development is the result of all the steps that have gone before, and that if any antecedent step had been different the world would not now be in its present condition. It is in this admission of the doctrine of evolution that we have found the real point of affinity between the seemingly ruthless theory of modern science and the undoubtedly benevolent view of the psalmist of Israel. Looked at on only one side of their dimensions, both the one and the other are ruthless. Each of them recognises the fact that there is an element of destruction in the world, and that in the development of that world there are things which go to the wall. But both, on the other hand, are agreed in maintaining that the destructive element has tended not to death but to life, that the seeming and temporary waste has issued in a state of higher development which without it would not have been, and that the epoch of ultimate perfection shall be found, when it is reached, to have been the direct result of all those epochs of imperfection which went before.

Strange as it may seem, then, the instinct of the earliest religious sentiment is at one with the ripest conclusion of modern science on the subject of this world's destiny. They are both agreed in affirming that the prospect of the world is on the whole optimistic. They both look forward to a time when the social fabric shall be perfected and the faculties of man shall be matured, and they both regard that time as having its present preparation in those very struggles and imperfections which to the eye of the pessimist seem to point to a contrary conclusion. But it is here that there opens up a question of great importance and significance both in the view of ethics and in the light of religion. The psalmist and the scientist are at one in the hope that the present struggle for existence shall issue in the survival of something more stable in its elements than the things which now exist. But are they agreed as to what it is that shall survive? The expressions associated with the doctrine of evolution are, "The survival of the strongest," and "The survival of the fittest." It is commonly thought that these expressions imply a theory; in truth, they state nothing. To say that one thing survives another, is simply in other words to say that one thing is stronger than another, for it can only have survived by reason of a greater strength. To affirm that I shall live longer than you, is simply to state in other words that I am more fitted than you for the conditions of this present life, for it is only on the ground of such superior fitness that any one life can outlast another. We repeat, therefore, that the so-called theory of evolution on the nature of survival does not pretend to be a theory at all. It simply declares the fact that in the struggle for existence there are some things which live and some things which die; it is a mere truism to add that the things which live are stronger and fitter for existence than the things which die. Modern science has made no attempt to define the nature of survival, no effort to indicate what is that element in certain lives which prolongs them beyond the term of others. It has paused at the statement of the truth that certain creatures are more adapted than others to the changes of climate and environment, and it leaves the secret of their adaptation a question still unsolved.

But if science has no theory as to what constitutes the power of survival, the religious sentiment of the Book of Psalms has a very distinct and a very decided theory. The psalmist of Israel, like the scientist of modern days, believes that the deaths of the world are making room for its more permanent life; but the psalmist of Israel holds on his way where the scientist breaks off. He professes to tell us not only that death is making room for a more permanent life, but what is the nature of that life which is to enjoy such a survival. He tells us that the life which in the struggle for existence is to survive all other lives is goodness. He looks forward to the establishment of a kingdom which shall never be moved, but he declares the reason of its immovableness to be the spirit of purity. He will not fear though the earth be removed and the mountains be cast into the midst of the sea, but his fearlessness is not on account of any superior outward advantages, but simply and solely because his refuge and his strength is God.

Here, then, is a new phase of the subject which in the light of modern evolution requires to be considered. That the righteous are to be the survivors, that the upright are to inherit the land, that the good are to obtain the blessing of ultimate prosperity, are statements which to the modern ear sound startling enough. Lord Bacon has somewhere said that prosperity is the blessing of the Old Testament, adversity the blessing of the New. The aphorism is designed to suggest that the Old Testament conception is a crude one, incidental to the stage of an early epoch. It seems to us that the Old Testament conception is that which belongs to all epochs whether early or late. Finely antithetical as is the saying of Bacon, it is profoundly untrue. Adversity is not the blessing of the New Testament; adversity is never a blessing. To wander "in the wilderness in a solitary way," to find "no city to dwell in," to sit "in darkness and in the shadow of death," to be "bound in affliction and iron,"—these are experiences which no religion, either Judaic or Christian, would pronounce to be in themselves desirable. Christianity proclaims the doctrine of the Cross; but why? Not certainly for its own sake, but for the sake of a crown which it is supposed to yield. Paul glories in tribulation, not because tribulation is glorious, but because it works out a far more exceeding and eternal weight of glory. It is no use, therefore, to charge the Old Testament conception with crudeness. If it be crude, it must share that reproach with all religion, for every religion in the world is based upon the attempt to find some relief from the pains of life; Buddhism itself is no exception. The simple question is whether this inevitable tendency of the religious sentiment be or be not consistent with the facts of life. The doctrine of evolution, as we have said, has proposed no counter-theory; do the *facts* of evolution suggest a counter-theory? Is there anything in our actual experience which militates against this ancient conclusion of the religious sentiment? The psalmist says that those who shall prosper in the end are the good, that those who shall flourish like the palm-tree are the righteous. He declares that they shall have in them so much of the principle of survival that they shall bring forth fruit in old age, shall reveal the strength of life at a time when other things experience the sense of decay. Has that conclusion become superannuated by the results of modern experience? It is not precluded by the theory of evolution in the abstract, but is it contradicted by the course of evolution in the world? That is the question which has to be met and pondered by him who would thoroughly estimate the relation between the science of the present and the religious sentiment of the past. A consideration of this subject will engage us in the following chapter.

CHAPTER IX.

THE PSALMIST'S PRINCIPLE OF SURVIVAL.

PSALMS ii., lxxii., xcii.

WE have placed these three psalms together because they represent one and the same phase of the Judaic religious sentiment. They may be called distinctively, Psalms of Survival. They describe the principle on which, according to the view of the Old Testament, the continuance of the world was to be prolonged. It will be seen at the outset that there is one thing on which the psalmist and the scientist are agreed; they both hold that the value of any object depends upon the length of its duration. Modern science declares that the things which survive are the fittest things in the universe; the psalmist of Israel affirms that the things which survive are the most favoured things in the universe. There is perfect agreement, therefore, as to the value assigned to the fact of long life. The agreement is all the more remarkable because a contrary idea has generally prevailed throughout ancient religions. Neither the Brahman nor the Buddhist would for a moment have admitted that the value of an object was to be determined by the length of its duration. The Buddhist would have made a directly opposite assertion. He would have declared that the value of an object was to be tested not by the length but by the brevity of its duration, and that the things most to be esteemed in the world were those which passed soonest into forgetfulness. But the Jew estimated everything by its power to live. That which passed into Nirvana was to him on that very account unworthy to be; it had proved its unfitness for the divine economy by its inability to keep its being. The modern scientist is here at one with the Jew, and singularly enough he is almost at one with him in terms; the Jew makes the survival a matter of divine election, the scientist makes it a matter of natural selection. The idea at the root of both conceptions is essentially the same—the ascription to the longest-lived of the highest place in the order of nature.

But now we come to a point in which the Jew and the scientist seem to part company. The Jew believes in the survival of the fittest, but he repudiates again and again the notion that the fittest means the physically strongest. This is somewhat remarkable. The Jew is supposed to be a man devoted to the physical, and it must be confessed that his creed bears in many points the impress of the sensuous. And yet, with all his tendency towards the physical, he has refused to accept the physical as his ideal of immortality, has refused to admit that the possession of outward strength can for a moment give to any being the claim to outlast his fellows. That the race is not to the swift nor the battle to the strong, that a king is not saved by the multitude of his host, that there is no trust to be placed in princes merely on the ground of their imperialism, is a sentiment that runs like a refrain through all his meditations. Judaism, the religion of the external, the religion of forms and shadows, the religion of rites and ceremonies, has yet been able throughout all her history to transcend her practice in her ideal. Following rigidly the order of her material institutions, and attaching herself so closely to the outward form as to be in danger of obliterating the spirit, she has yet never for an hour lost sight of that spirit as the only source of ultimate survival, has never for an instant ceased to maintain that all flesh is grass, and all materialism but the flower of the field, and that the only thing which shall live for ever is the breath of the spirit of life.

This thought appears very strikingly in these three psalms which we have taken as the mottoes of this chapter. Ps. ii. has always been regarded as a prophecy of the Messiah. In scientific language, it is a statement by the Jewish writer of what constitutes, in his view, the principle of survival. It is quite clear that in his view the principle of survival is not physical strength. He looks forward to a kingdom which has physical strength for its adversary, and which is to establish its dominion by the vanquishing of that strength. The heathen are represented as raging, the people as imagining a vain or sensuous thing. The kings of the earth stand up, and the rulers take counsel together to crush out the spark of spirituality from the world. During all this time the spark of spirituality never flickers. Over against the attitude of physical strength there stands an attitude of calm repose. The divine spirit which is to conquer the world is represented as looking on the accumulated forces of the physical with an unconcern amounting to disdain: "Why do the heathen rage, and the people imagine a vain thing?" It is represented as so unconcerned as to be at first unwilling even to take action against the adversary, and to be disposed to meet that adversary rather with a smile of contempt than with a rod of iron: "He that sitteth in the heavens shall laugh: the Lord shall have them in derision." The very attitude expressed in the word "sitteth" is that of conscious strength absolutely unperturbed by the threatened opposition. And if there follows a burst of indignation and a blast of divine anger, it is an anger which endures but for a moment, and is itself followed in turn by a restoration of the calm; the threat to break with the rod of iron and dash in pieces like a potter's vessel, is quickly succeeded by the gentle invitation, "Kiss the Son, lest He be angry, and ye perish from the way."

All this points conclusively to the thought not only that the spiritual Messianic kingdom is confident of its victory over materialism, but that it is confident of winning that victory through purely spiritual weapons. The peaceful character of this kingdom is even more clearly marked in Ps. lxxii. That psalm is designed to describe the advent of a glorious empire whose dominion is to stretch from sea to sea. But its glory is a purely spiritual glory. Its blessedness consists not in the fact that its dominion is illimitable and its duration everlasting, but in the fact that its reign is a refuge from oppression and its sway a protection from the forces of violence. Indeed the whole idea of the psalm is that its dominion is illimitable and its duration everlasting simply because it is a spiritual empire. The leading thought in the mind of the psalmist is identical with that thought which under the shadows of Horeb dominated the spirit of Elijah—that the power of the still small voice, insignificant as it then seemed, had yet in it an element of strength which was fitted at once to survive and to conquer the thunder and the earthquake and the fire. It is on the ground of this spirituality, on the ground of this capacity to calm the turbulent forces of the world, that the psalmist ascribes to the Messianic kingdom an extent of sway and a permanence of duration which no kingdom of the world had hitherto enjoyed. "His name shall endure for ever: His name shall be continued as long as the sun: and men shall be blessed in Him: all nations shall call Him blessed."

Turning now to Psalm xcii. we meet precisely the same thought. The recurrence of the thought is a matter well worth observing, because it shows that this conception of the Messianic kingdom is not the conception of an individual mind, but a distinctly national idea emanating from the very heart of Judaism. In the 92d Psalm there are present to the vision of the seer two forces, the one animal, the other spiritual. The line of contrast is clearly drawn in verses 5 and 6: "O Lord, Thy thoughts are very deep. A brutish man knoweth not; neither doth a fool understand this." The antithesis is evidently between the power of the spiritual and the power of the animal life. The former is already contemplated as superior to the latter, but its superiority is not yet recognised. The brutish life has at present possession of the field, and through its very incapacity to understand the life of spirit, it crushes and oppresses it. The psalmist is vividly alive to the fact that to the eye of any observer it would appear as if the animal life had the best of it in this world, but he declares that the very circumstance of its coming first to the front is itself a proof of its want of permanence. "When the wicked spring as the grass, and when all the workers of iniquity do flourish; it is that they shall be destroyed for ever." The idea seems to be analogous to that in the parable of the sower, where a certain kind of seed springs up rapidly just because it has no deepness of earth. The animal impulses are earlier in their manifestation than the spiritual impulses, and because they are earlier in their manifestation they are naturally more suited to rule the earlier stages of development. The spirit comes upon the scene originally as an intruder and an interloper; it is a stranger in a strange land, and can as yet claim no possession in it. That is not first which is spiritual, but that which is natural. Yet in this region as in most others, the saying remains true that the last shall be first. The spiritual life is not adapted to the primitive stages of development, and therefore during these primitive stages it is overborne by the life of nature. But just on that account it prophesies for itself a longer survival, because it proves itself to belong to a more developed age. It is the messenger which the coming era sends to prepare the way before it, and it looks for the manifestation of its strength, not to the immediate world in which it dwells, but to the advent of the world from which it comes. This is the true ground of the psalmist's confidence in the survival of the spiritual over the material. He expresses the fact of that survival in the most unqualified terms when he says of the citizens of the future kingdom, "They shall still bring forth fruit in old age." He designs to mark his conviction that the strength of the Messianic kingdom shall not consist in the materials which are called physical, but shall be able to subsist even in the dearth of these materials. It is a thought strongly analogous to that which breaks forth in the words of the prophet: "Even the youths shall faint and grow weary, and the young men shall utterly fall: but they that wait upon the Lord shall renew their strength;" "they shall run, and not be weary; they shall walk, and not faint."

This Messianic kingdom is to the mind of the Jew not a mere abstraction; it centres in an individual life, an ideal man. The eye of prophet and psalmist is riveted not on a race but on a person. The historical character of the kingdom is marked by the fact that it is to find its beginning in the life of a single soul. The Man to whom the aspiration of Judaism looks forward as the goal of its hopes is distinctively a spiritual man. He is one who shall not strive nor cry, whose voice shall not be heard in the streets, who shall grow up gently as a tender plant. He is one whose aspect shall not be deemed beautiful when measured by the standard of the physical forces, whose beauty shall be despised and rejected by the culture of a previous age. And yet, to the view of the Israelite the kingdom which this new life is to inaugurate is not a supernatural kingdom; it is rather a gathering into unity of those elements of nature which are now repressed and overshadowed. Judaism had three great ideals which she longed to see realised; she was in search of a prophet, a priest, and a king. She had in her community men professing to represent each of these offices, but nowhere was her ideal realised. Her prophets, her priests, and her kings were not yet men of the spirit; they were only men of the body. Their empire rested mainly on physical conditions. Her prophet was a man who could unveil the events of the future, who could rend asunder the curtain of to-morrow and render visible those acts and issues now buried in uncertainty. Her priest was a man who could offer up visible victims, who could exhibit the spectacle of sacrifices distinguished by their manifestation of physical pain. Her king was a man who could rule by outward force, who could dominate by the power of the sword, and govern by the numbering of armies. In the course of her actual experience Israel had not seen the threefold functions of her government more than physically realised.

But the realisation which Israel wanted was a spiritual one. She desired to see these three offices lifted out of the sphere of a barren materialism and transplanted into the world of mind. She looked for a prophet who should be able to reveal not merely the visible acts of to-morrow, but the invisible principles which are the same yesterday, and to-day, and for ever. She looked for a priest who should be able to offer not merely the pain and cries of a physical victim, but the will and love of a self-surrendering spirit. She looked for a king who should be able to rule not simply by stretching out the rod of an outward dominion, but by stooping to the wants and bearing the weaknesses of his people—for a king whose empire should be built on the foundations of priesthood, and whose throne should be established on the steps of sacrifice. This was the ideal which dominated over the heart and floated before the eyes of the Jewish nation. She never lost sight of it even in her darkest hour—nay, it was the sight of it that often enabled her to survive that darkness. In proportion as her past receded from her, the prospect of her future glory appeared more near. She left ever farther behind those glories of the age of Solomon which at one time had promised to be the actual coming of the kingdom. Her unity was broken into fragments, and her families were dispersed among the nations, and between herself and her former splendour there stood the barred gate guarded by the cherubim and the flaming sword. But it was just in this hour that the hope of Israel burned most brightly. It was just in this hour that there began to break upon her the thought that adversity and not prosperity was to be the dawn of her day of glory. It was in her season of darkness that there came before her prophetic vision the sight of a sinless "servant of God," who should sprinkle all nations, just because His visage was more marred than the children of men, and who should divide the spoil with the strong because He had poured forth his soul unto death. In her day of deepest gloom, Israel caught sight of the truth that the force which was to survive all other forces was that very power of spiritual endurance which, to the eye of contemporary nations, appeared of all others the weakest, the most despicable thing.

It may be said, What has all this to do with science? what, especially, has it to do with the science of our day? Is not the modern doctrine of evolution based on a serious of facts which are in direct antagonism to the ideal of ancient Israel? Would it not be bound to regard this religious sentiment of the past as simply a product of sentimentality? The religious sentiment of ancient Israel is based upon the belief that the spiritual forces shall conquer the physical, and that the sacrificial forces shall ultimately be the survivors of all. Is not the modern doctrine of evolution founded on the observation of facts which point to an exactly opposite conclusion? Does it not rest on the conviction that might is the strongest force in the universe, and that those creatures whose physical organisation is most powerful must obtain the victory and the survival over those whose bodily structure is weak?

Such, indeed, is a very common view of those facts which bear upon the modern doctrine of evolution; and if it be the true one, it is certainly in diametrical opposition to the religious sentiment of ancient Israel. But is it the true one? We are convinced, for our part, that it is not. We believe that if the modern system of evolution be examined, it will be found to point to a conclusion essentially the same as that which in another sphere was reached by the Jewish psalmist. Looked at from the outside, it seems to the eye of an observer as if the history of evolution were the history of that process by which physical strength preys upon physical debility. But let us remember that, in the history of evolution as in the realm of nature itself, the strength of a physical organisation is accompanied by a strength which is not physical, by a power of force which is inward. We are not here discussing the question whether the principle which we call life be or be not the result of physical organisation. We take our present stand on a position which materialism itself will not contest. From whatever source life has proceeded, it will not be denied that it actually manifests a series of effects entirely different in their appearance from the appearance of those effects produced by material mechanism. It is in order to mark this difference that all men of every school have agreed to call the one inward and the other outward. Taking our stand on this universal admission, we are bound to recognise the fact that every development of physical organisation is accompanied by a development of vital power. Recognising this fact, we are compelled to take a different view of the order of evolution in the world. We are no longer entitled to say that the history of evolution is the history of physical strength preying on physical weakness. If the strength of physical organisation is accompanied by a corresponding strength of life, we are bound to take into the account the latter as well as the former factor. Conceding that the stronger physical organisation obtains the victory over the weaker, it still remains to be determined whether it obtains that victory by reason of that which is physical or by reason of that which is vital —whether, to use the Scriptural alternative,[1] its ascendancy is acquired by outward might and power, or by that increase of the spiritual element which has might and power for its environment. If that by which the stronger conquer the weaker is not the strength of their body but the strength of their life, the history of evolution will still be the history of the victory of spirit over matter, and the verdict of

[1] Zech. iv. 6.

the Gentile apostle will be confirmed by modern science, that the weak things of the world have been chosen to confound the things that are strong.

Now, is there any evidence for this position? Is there any proof in nature that the force by which the physically strong overcome the physically weak is essentially a spiritual force? in other words, that they overcome by reason of that strength which developed organisation gives to spirit? It seems to us that there is—that even that sphere which we call animal nature is the record of the warfare by which life dominates matter. We have simply to consider what a great element in the promotion of survival is the actual intelligence that resides in the animal life. We use the word "intelligence" advisedly. It is a great mistake to imagine that all the acts of animal foresight are performed by the power of what we call blind instinct. Instinct only extends to some particular forms of animal action; intelligence, as well as instinct, has its part to play. Nay, in the view of the modern evolutionist, what we call instinct is itself only the crystallisation into a habit of what was once a conscious and voluntary action, only the power to do a thing spontaneously from the fact that, through a series of generations, an effort has been made to do it with design. But if it be so, what follows? Clearly this, that one of the greatest agents in the promotion of animal survival is an agency of the nature of mind, a force which has acquired instinctive power simply by reason of its long-continued exercise. Those acts by which the animal provides for its daily subsistence, and makes provision for the sustenance of its offspring, are, in the view of the modern evolutionist, acts which, just because they are instinctive, mark the development of an inward vital power which has obtained the victory over forces merely mechanical.

If we turn to another department of the evolutionary field, the sphere of sexual selection, we shall see yet more clearly an illustration of this principle. Sexual selection is admittedly one of the most powerful agencies of natural selection. It would be impossible for the fittest to survive unless there were in the animal world some bond of attraction, either between the fittest and the fittest, or between the less fit and the more fit. Fitness can only be preserved by a principle of heredity, and the principle of heredity demands that the stronger creatures of creation should have their strength so recognised as to make them eligible to the other sex. Now we find that, as a matter of fact, there are in the animal world certain things which constitute a bond of sexual attraction. We find in some instances that one bird is attracted to another by the beauty of its plumage; in others by the sweetness of its song. But have we considered how much is implied in this simple and familiar fact? Have we considered that in each of these instances the agency which really promotes survival is an agency not of matter, but of mind? The beauty of plumage is something physical, but the power to be attracted by that beauty is not physical at all. The sweetness of song has partly its source in mechanical causes, but the susceptibility of being influenced by that sweetness has nothing to do with mechanism, it is the property of life alone. How, then, comes it that the beauty of a bird's plumage or the sweetness of a bird's song constitutes to its comrade a source of attraction? It is clear that it can only do so because there is at work an agency other than its own, an agency which cannot be described by any analogy of material mechanism, and which, therefore, we habitually attribute to life itself. The power which renders the bird of beautiful plumage and the bird of sweet song fitted to survive is the susceptibility of certain stages of the animal life for beholding beauty. There is nothing in beautiful plumage, nor in sweetness of song, which should make either of them fitted to survive. Why should an ungainly appearance or a discordant mode of utterance be less suited to a long life than an aspect of gracefulness or a tone of sweetness? Considering these things in themselves, there is manifestly no reason whatever why the one should live longer than the other. But then it so happens that we are not called to consider them in themselves. Bright plumage and sweet song would be no more fit to live than their contraries but for the fact that there are certain creatures which have a tendency to love brightness, and certain creatures which have a tendency to admire sweet sounds. It is the relation of these things to others which makes them fit objects for survival; the beautiful is preserved from death because it appeals to a sense of beauty. But let us consider what this amounts to; nothing less than this, that even in the sensuous and animal creation the fitness of an object for survival depends upon its correspondence with a want of the inward life. The real agent in the process is not a force of mechanism, but an incipient force of mind, the beginning of that æsthetic tendency which ultimately develops into the sense of beauty.

Here already, within the precincts of the animal world, we are brought into contact with that principle which is destined to play so prominent a part in the annals of the Jewish nation, "The elder shall serve the younger." The meaning of that principle is not difficult to read. It designs to express the fact that the forces which are later in their development, and which are originally weaker in their manifestation, shall ultimately conquer and surpass the forces which preceded them in time and at first triumphed over them. It is to illustrate this principle that the posterity of Seth are made to excel the posterity of Cain, Isaac to outrun Ishmael, and Jacob to take the precedence of Esau. But it is less frequently observed that the principle here enunciated is precisely the same law which operates in the world of evolution. The principle of divine election in the Old Testament is identical with the law of natural selection in the sphere of nature. In the latter equally as in the former case, the elder serves the younger, the forces later and originally weaker obtain the victory over those primitive powers which, because they were first in the field, began by overshadowing them. In the present instance we see this singularly illustrated. The sense of beauty is not an instinct of primitive life, not a power which necessarily belongs to the vital principle. In the earliest epochs of the world it would assuredly have found itself out of place, would have been amongst those things of which it was said, "To what purpose is this waste?" The sense of beauty would have been completely surpassed in the race for primitive existence. It would have been surpassed because there would have been no interest in that which was its object. Beautiful forms would not have been valued on account of their beauty, nor on account of their beauty would they have been preserved; if preserved, they must have owed their survival to some additional element. But with the later development of the animal world, this very principle, which originally finds no recognition, becomes a main factor in the progress of life. It not only ceases to be surpassed by the earlier and more mechanical forces, but it begins gradually to take the precedence over these forces, and ultimately acquires an influence to which there is scarcely a rival. The last has become the first, and the elder serves the younger.

When we pass from the animal to the human we find this law enunciated in its most pronounced and unqualified form. The writer of the Book of Genesis speaks of man as the being who was to have dominion over all other creatures. And yet, to one who was privileged to be a spectator of the earliest form of human life, nothing would have seemed more unlikely than the fulfilment of such a prophecy. At whatever stage and in whatever method man entered upon the scene, he entered upon the scene with a force apparently weaker than those forces which he came to displace, and which he professed to rule over. In all physical characteristics he was decidedly inferior to the creatures which preceded him on the stage of time. He did not possess the strength of the lion, nor the swiftness of the roe, nor the eye of the eagle. He was deficient in those instincts which, almost by a mechanical power, had guided the lower creation in the provision for its daily wants. It is true he brought into life powers which the lower creation did not possess; but it seemed for the present as if these were precisely the powers which could bring no possible advantage to an occupant of this world, which would contribute rather to retard than to accelerate the progress of vital development. It was to this creature, so unlikely to reign, so likely to be crushed, that the promise was given by the writer of Genesis, " Have dominion over the fish of the sea, and over the fowl of the air, and over every living thing that moveth upon the earth." Nay, the promise was more unlikely and more paradoxical still. Not only was man, though physically the weakest product of creation, to obtain the empire over all his forerunners, but he was to obtain that empire through that which was physically weakest in himself. That which was to bruise the head of the serpent was the seed of the woman; the animal forces of the past were to be crushed by that force in man which of all others is furthest removed from the exertion of animal strength. The power which was to vanquish the principalities and thrones of an earlier age was precisely that power which in an earlier age would by reason of its weakness have been unable to subsist for an hour. This, and nothing less than this, is the bold thought which confronts us on the opening page of the Jewish Scriptures, and which runs like a thread of gold through its every subsequent page. It is the subject of historians, it is the theme of prophets, it is the song of psalmists. And as it meets us at the opening of the Old Testament, it confronts us also at its close—on that mountain of Beatitudes which was to supersede the mountain of Sinai. Here it is once more declared that the principle of survival which had dominated the old covenant was itself to survive its dissolution, and that in the new dispensation which was about to dawn, the seed of the woman was still to bruise the head of the serpent. The poor in spirit were to receive the kingdom, the meek were to inherit the earth, the peacemakers were to be called the children of God.

Nor was this latest utterance of the Scripture prophecy less unlikely in itself than the earlier one. If it seemed a paradox at the beginning of human existence that the seed of the woman should bruise the head of the serpent, it certainly must have seemed no less paradoxical that the future empire of the world should be swayed by Christian meekness. At the time when that prophecy was uttered the empires of the world were in point of fact swayed by brute force. The kingdoms of the earth were not ruled by the poor in spirit but by the proud in heart. The men who were esteemed the sons of God were not the makers of peace but the makers of war. The heroism to which was promised the inheritance of supreme dominion was not the meekness which could shed its own blood, but the violence which could shed the blood of its enemies. To a spectator of the new creation as to a spectator of the old, the promise on the Mount of Beatitudes must have appeared of all things the wildest, the most unsubstantial dream. When the Divine Founder of Christianity cast His eye upon His insignificant company and said, "Fear not, little flock, for it is your Father's good pleasure to give you the kingdom," He said something more unlikely to be fulfilled than if he had foretold the occurrence of any special event; He uttered a prediction which could only be accomplished by the occurrence and the convergence of a whole series of events distinctively special and pre-eminently peculiar.

But the most remarkable circumstance is that the prediction has been fulfilled. The forces which have survived the dissolution of the Roman empire have been precisely those forces which the Roman empire deemed unworthy to live, precisely that poverty of spirit, meekness, mercifulness, and peacefulness which to the mind of that contemporaneous world were of all things the most contemptible and vanishing. It is true that in modern Christendom we find instances of violence and brutality as great as was ever exhibited by ancient paganism; we can still say of Christ, as was said by the writer to the Hebrews, "We see not yet all things subject unto Him." But what marks the transition between the old life and the new is the displacement of the old ideal. The ideal of an age is ever the forerunner of its practice, and where its ideal is changed the change of its practice is sure to follow. The ideal of the old Roman age is dead in modern Christendom. Modern Christians do not, any more than ancient pagans, always exhibit the spirit of meekness and mercy; but modern Christians feel what ancient pagans did not—that in failing to exhibit that spirit they are falling beneath the standard of true men. The most dangerous feature about ancient Rome was not so much its deeds of violence as its admiration of those deeds. That head of the serpent which the seed of the woman was to bruise is not a thing but a thought. The practice of the ancient world was simply the outward expression of its theory, and its theory was the direct result of its ideal of greatness. Its ideal of greatness was the real serpent's head. It followed the paths of violence because it viewed the paths of violence as the road to heroism; it pursued the practice of brute force because it looked upon brute force as the highest manifestation of power which the visible universe revealed. It was impossible to effect a revolution at any other point than the fountain-head, and the fountain-head was the thought. To change the manners of the old world it was inevitable that first of all its ideal of greatness should be changed. It must be shown that brute force was not the highest manifestation of power, it must be taught that to conquer by violence is not the greatest triumph of man. This is what Christianity has already done. Other parts of its work are still in the future, but this is completed now. The serpent has been bruised in its *head*. The animal has ceased to be an object of worship. It still survives in human nature, but it no longer survives in human admiration; it bruises still the heel of humanity, but it has lost its influence over the brain.

It may be said that all this belongs to the sphere of the pulpit, that it may be edifying to the preacher, but is not matter for the scientist. In truth, however, the facts here adduced are peculiarly scientific facts. They have doubtless an interest for the preacher and for the religious mind in general, but their special importance is for the evolutionist. The evolutionist, as we have seen, has promulgated the doctrine that the fittest survive, without having ventured to define what constitutes the fitness for survival. The psalmist has ventured to offer such a definition: he has declared that the kingdom which is to sway all other kingdoms is an empire of spiritual morality, of sacrificial love. Christianity in the fulness of time has proclaimed itself to be the realisation of that kingdom, and has asserted in yet more pronounced terms its destiny to inherit the earth. Modern civilisation has already fulfilled that promise. The power of Christianity has penetrated far beyond the reception of its doctrines, and even those who reject its doctrines are professedly influenced by its power. Its power is as yet chiefly mental. It has not transformed the world's practice, it has only transformed its ideal; but the world's ideal is the head of the serpent, and where the head of the serpent is bruised, its body cannot long survive. These are the facts, and, if they are received as facts at all, they must be accepted as facts of science. The religion of the psalmist, which is in germ the religion of Christ, comes to us here not as the antagonist but as the supplement of scientific thought. It builds upon the lines of the student of evolution, without being itself conscious that it is so doing. It utters speech precisely at that point where science is forced to keep silence: it offers an answer to that question which science has left unanswered. It accepts the conclusion of science, that there are some forms in this world which are more fitted to survive than other forms; but it goes on to tell us what science leaves untold—the nature of that which constitutes fitness for life. It tells us that the name which shall endure for ever is a name which symbolises sacrifice, which expresses moral beauty, which personifies perfect purity. It declares that the kingdom which shall rule all other kingdoms is an empire built upon the throne of mercy, of meekness, and of justice, and that the weapons which shall make the men of the future the sons of God, shall be the weapons not of war but of peace. When we add to all this the fact that historical experience has confirmed its testimony, and that the unlikely prophecy has been and is still being wondrously fulfilled, we have found on one field at least of evolution a meeting-place with the faith of Christendom, and have proved the hope of the ancient psalmist to have been a scientific hope.

CHAPTER X.

THE PSALMIST'S PRINCIPLE OF SURVIVAL.
(*Continued.*)

PSALM i.

IN the previous chapter we arrived at the conclusion that on one fundamental question there is an agreement between the verdict of the religious sentiment and the verdict of scientific research. We found that the psalmist and the scientist are at one in holding that there is a principle of fitness in the universe which enables certain things to live longer than other things. We found on further examination that the apparent contrariety between them as to the nature of those things which survive is not a real contrariety. The psalmist looks for the establishment of a spiritual kingdom; the scientist apparently arrives at the conclusion that the history of the course of nature is the history of that process by which the strong vanquish the weak. We found, however, that even from a scientific standpoint this is not the history of the course of nature, and that the process which evolution reveals is precisely the process which the psalmist contemplated. We saw that when in nature the strong conquer the weak it is not on account of their superior strength but on account of their superior spirituality, that they obtain the victory over their predecessors in the field because by reason of a higher inward principle they are really more emancipated from the dominion of matter. By the verdict, therefore, alike of religion and of science, the principle of survival is the principle of spirituality, and the forms which have survived the longest are those forms in which the spiritual element has most fully subordinated and dominated the physical forces. The latest survivors in the world have been the sacrificial lives, the lives which in their own individual nature have allowed the spirit to obtain the victory over the flesh, and the prophecy of the Sermon on the Mount has become almost a fact in the field of evolution, "Blessed are the meek, for they shall inherit the earth."

Thus far the religious sentiment is in harmony with the conclusions of modern science. But we now go on to take a further step in the elucidation of this inquiry. The psalmist declares that the principle of survival by which spirit outlives matter has its ultimate ground in morality. He declares that it is not merely a fact of nature but a fact of divine retribution, that it is only a law of nature because it is in conformity with the law of God. The question is here shifted on to a higher ground, and we are required to look at it from a loftier and a more difficult standpoint. Science will be quite ready to admit that, as a matter of fact, the sacrificial life has been gradually gaining the advantage in the world, but it will insist on explaining this by purely scientific causes. The psalmist, on the other hand, insists on explaining it by causes which are purely moral. He would be quite ready to admit that it is a law of science or of physical nature, but he would maintain that it has only become so because it is a divine law. In the psalm which we have placed at the head of this chapter the fundamental idea is that the survival of the fittest is the survival of those who are most in conformity with the will of God; and as this psalm is generally regarded as a preface to the whole book, its sentiment may be taken as representing the common thought of Jewish devotion. It brings before us two classes—those who are blessed, and those who are not blessed. The blessedness of the former consists in the fact that their life shall not be evanescent; that they shall be like a tree planted by a river, and shall have a leaf that will not fade. The unblessedness of the latter consists in the fact that their life *shall* be evanescent; that they shall be like the chaff which the wind driveth away, that their "way shall perish." The element of blessedness therefore is, in the view of the psalmist, the capacity for survival; the element of unblessedness, the incapacity. But the psalmist goes on to tell us that this blessedness has its ground not in a physical, but in a moral cause. The man who survives for ever does so because "his delight is in the law of the Lord"; the man who vanishes like chaff driven by the wind does so because he is "ungodly." The ultimate ground of eternal life, therefore, is here placed in a moral distinction, and the principle of survival shades into a higher principle—the law of retribution.

Now there is no subject on which the present age is thought to be more utterly divided from the past than the belief in that theory called the law of retribution. The nineteenth century is pre-eminently an age of law; its leading aim is to reduce everything to law. The days of the psalmist were in one respect analogous. The ancient Israelite, like the modern scientist, not only believed in the existence of an unchanging and unchangeable law, but he believed that within the compass of this law every object in heaven and earth must somehow be included. But the difference between the ancient Israelite and the modern scientist lies here: the former looked upon law as itself a product; the latter regards it as an ultimate scientific fact. The modern scientist, as a scientist, never asks why things are so; the ancient Israelite never ceases to ask that question. The one regards law as simply the constitution of nature; the other views it as an expression of Divine will. Hence, to the one, the conception of law is the conception of something which is essentially physical; to the other, it is the recognition of something which is emphatically spiritual. To the Hebrew mind every law is a law of retribution. Everything is what it is simply because God made it so, and God made it so with a human reference. Light is sown for the righteous, and joy for the upright in heart. The economy of the universe is a government in which the good man prospers and the evil man perishes. The one is heir to the kingdom of God and all its glories; the other is excluded from that kingdom and debarred from its glories. The kingdom of God is not a future world, but the enjoyment of the present world; its glories are not crowns and harps above, but wealth and possessions below. When therefore it is said that the good man inherits the kingdom, it is thereby implied that his life shall be one of prosperity, that his cup shall be running over with all natural as well as with all spiritual blessings, and that he shall find an abundant reward in the success of his earthly labours.

Now here is the point in which the spirit of modern science seems to join issue with the spirit of ancient Israel. Agreeing with the ancient Israelite in the desire to reduce everything within the dimensions of an unchanging law, the modern scientist refuses to follow him when he declares that law to be retributive. The law of nature as expounded by the modern scientist, so far from being a law of retribution, is one that is indifferent to moral distinctions. In the strictest sense of the word it is no respecter of persons. It makes its sun to rise upon the evil and upon the good, without discriminating between their evil and their goodness. It would not indorse the distinction drawn by the writer of the first psalm. It would freely admit that to be planted by rivers of water and to have a leaf that does not fade, is a more blessed state of being than to be like the chaff which the wind drives away; but it would emphatically deny that the difference between these states is a difference which originates in divine retribution. Divine retribution is in fact the one idea which the spirit of our age pronounces unscientific. It declares that the facts of nature as observed by human experience do not warrant the conclusion that a man is rewarded for keeping the law or punished for breaking it. It points to a multitude of cases in which the good man seems to be driven like the chaff before the wind, and in which the wicked man appears to be planted by the rivers of water. Its very doctrine of the survival of the strongest is, as popularly interpreted, a denial of the doctrine that the fate of men is regulated by the proportion of their good or evil.

Is, then, the Bible theory of retribution doomed to be an obsolete belief? Are we compelled henceforth, in the interests of modern science, to abandon that conclusion of the religious sentiment which saw in the smiles of fortune a result of divine favour, and in its frowns an evidence of divine aversion? Let us remember that the difficulty is not purely a modern one. The Bible itself recognises it. The same Book of Psalms which at one time rejoices in the manifest congruity between a man's fortune and his character, at another is oppressed with the thought that the wicked are allowed to spread like a green bay-tree. The Book of Job expresses the struggle of the human mind with precisely the same problem—the problem why a good man should be afflicted above men who do not share his goodness. Yet it is worthy of remark, that although Judaism felt the modern difficulty it never accepted the modern solution. The psalmist might fret because of the prosperity of evil-doers, but he comforted himself with the thought that by-and-by there would come a change; the writer of the Book of Job might lament the arbitrary inequalities which for a time disfigured life, but he saw at the close of his drama a restitution of happiness to the good. They did not solve the problem, they did not try to solve it. Even the Book of Job does not attempt to clear up the mystery which it is written to evolve. It simply recognises the fact that in the long-run all shall be well with the righteous, and it is content to recognise it purely by an act of faith. There is no effort made to reconcile the final brightness with the present darkness: the presence of the darkness is freely admitted, but a solace is found in the hope that ultimately it will vanish in perfect day. The question is, Is there any scientific ground for this hope? It was accepted by psalmists and prophets on grounds not of science but of faith. Is there anything in the conclusions of modern science which makes it impossible to hold this faith? Has our age passed into a view of nature which is no longer compatible with the acceptance of a creed wherein the law is benevolent to the good and adverse to the bad? Has the scientific sentiment banished that phase of the religious sentiment which led men to see in the actual world the presence and the power of a retributive justice?

Now, strange as it may seem, we venture to affirm that this phase of the ancient religious sentiment is capable of being transplanted into the domain of modern science. In spite of appearances to the contrary, we feel convinced that the ideas embodied in the first psalm are susceptible of being embodied in the creed of evolution, and that the notion of retribution may still be incorporated even in that conception of law which belongs to the scientist of the nineteenth century. And to bring out this point, let us for the sake of the argument adopt the scientific term for the name of God: instead of speaking of God, let us speak of Nature, and print the word with a capital. Spinoza is one of those who prefer to call God by the name Nature. He distinguishes two kinds of Nature—a Nature which is brought forth, and a Nature which brings forth. It is only the latter of these, however, which, strictly speaking, we are entitled to print with a capital. That which is brought forth is merely passive; it is not in any sense a principle of life, and therefore it is in no sense an origin of the universe. Let it be understood, then, that when we speak of Nature we mean Nature on its active side; we apply the word not to that which is brought forth but to that which brings forth. We may assume that, by the verdict alike of the scientist and the psalmist, there is in the universe an originating Power. It does not matter at present whether we regard that Power as existing behind the universe or as constituting the universe itself. The psalmist takes the former view, the scientist the latter; the psalmist, accordingly, calls the originating Power God, the scientist speaks of it as Nature. We shall not here dispute the point. The two names cover one fact; they both imply the existence of an originating element in the universe, and to this extent they indicate on the part of science and religion the acceptance of a common basis.

Let us now go a step further. Science admits that there exists an originating element in the universe, which it describes by the name of Nature, or that which brings forth. But science goes on to tell us something more. It not only admits the existence of an originating principle, but it professes to trace the rule according to which this principle acts—in other words, it investigates the *law* of Nature. A law in the language of science is a rule of action; when it speaks of a law of Nature it designs to indicate that the originating principle does not act arbitrarily but on certain definite lines. Now to this extent the doctrine of the psalmist is at one with the doctrine of the scientist. The God of the Old Testament is a much more theistic conception than the *Nature* of modern science; but they have both this in common, that neither of them acts arbitrarily. The God of the Old Testament has bound Himself by the law which He has made. He not only demands that His law shall be the rule according to which others shall act; He insists that it shall also be the rule of His own action. He elects to move within those lines in which He has chosen that His creatures shall move. He refuses to deviate from that path which He has ordained that others shall follow—in a word, He has made Himself subject to that law of universal government in which He has determined that all things shall live, and move, and have their being.

In science then, as in religion, there is an originating principle, and there is a rule according to which that originating principle acts; to express the same thing in other words, there is a law of Nature. We are now prepared to take a third step, which shall bring us still nearer to a conformity between them. Every transgression of the law of Nature is a source of pain. It is either accompanied by pain at the time, or it is followed by pain afterwards. It is, for example, one of the commandments of Nature's law that an object in this world shall gravitate towards the earth. Suppose that a man should attempt to break this commandment; suppose that instead of keeping his feet on the ground he should ascend a lofty eminence and leap into the air with the intention of flying, the result will be severe bodily injury, perhaps death. The pain incurred is the result of a law which has been broken, and is proportionate to the extent to which that law has been broken. This is a principle the truth of which will be freely admitted by modern science. Nay, modern science will go much further. It not only holds that the attempt to break a law of Nature involves pain, it maintains that all pain is the result of some interruption in the natural course of a living organism. Philosophically speaking, and scientifically speaking, pain is simply the protest of a living creature against a wrong state of things in its own constitution, simply an effort of the organism to get back into a right state of things. That is the reason why the experience of acute pain is often deemed a favourable symptom of disease; it indicates a tendency on the part of the patient to return to the normal condition of life. In every case the pain, from whatever source it comes, owes its existence to the fact that the organism has previously been in a state which is not compatible with the exercise of its normal functions; it is the retribution sent by Nature as the result of an interrupted development of its law.

Let us take yet another step. This definition of pain is precisely the sense in which the Bible understands retribution. The earliest statement of the Scriptural doctrine of retribution is contained in the words of Genesis ii. 17, "In the day that thou eatest thereof thou shalt surely die." It is popularly thought that the words are designed to imply a threat, that they owe their deepest significance to the menace which they contain of a divine penalty. This, however, is not the sense in which they were understood by St Paul, who, as a Jew, and one versed in the Scriptures of Judaism, may be accepted as a competent interpreter of the religious spirit of his nation. Paul says, "to be carnally minded *is* death." The idea clearly is that the passage in

Genesis owes its significance to the fact that it is not so much a threat as a warning; that it is not so much the record of a penalty which God shall inflict if men sin, as the indication of a danger which men will incur in the very act of sinning. When I say to the child, "If you go near the fire you will suffer," what do I mean? Do I intend to impress the child with the belief that in going near the fire it will expose itself to a penalty from me? No; what I want to convey is, that the character of fire is such as to involve immediate danger when in contact with a living organism. Now this, in the view of St Paul, is precisely the thought intended to be expressed by the writer of Genesis. When he says that the day of sinning shall be the day of death, he means to imply that fire burns, and that to go too near the fire is to incur the danger of being burned. To be carnally minded *is* death. The act of disobedience to a divine principle is not simply an act which lays itself open to divine punishment; it is an act which involves in itself a process of separation from the divine life, and which, therefore, carries in its bosom the experience of a present punishment. The truth is, the deepest idea of Scripture on this subject is not that of punishment, but of retribution. The words do not mean the same thing. A punishment is something which is sent as the result of personal demerit; a retribution is something which comes as the result of a broken law. If I fall from the top of a house and experience bodily injury, I cannot be said to have met with a punishment; my fall has been accidental, and therefore involves no demerit. None the less is my injury a retribution. It is the retribution which I have incurred by reason of breaking a law. If I had not broken the law of gravitation, this injury would not have befallen me; the law has, so to speak, avenged on me the fact of its violation. This, we say, is the Bible doctrine of retribution. Its doctrine is that the man who violates a law of Nature shall suffer through the very violation of that law, quite irrespectively of whether he has or has not meant to violate it. The whole essence of the Scriptural system lies in the belief that there is a natural sequence in the order of things, that there is a legitimate place which every object shall occupy in the universe, and that to effect, either voluntarily or involuntarily, the displacement of any object, is inevitably to expose ourselves to the experience of injury.

And it is here we are to look for the reason of a doctrine which has often appeared one of the most mysterious and inexplicable parts of the Old Testament system—the doctrine that the deeds of the fathers are visited upon the children. Men have talked much of the harshness and the cruelty of such a dispensation, and have pointed to the statement as a proof of the low condition of development in which such a notion originated. And yet, strange to say, the Jewish Scriptures are nowhere in more strict harmony with the most advanced stages of development, nowhere in more perfect agreement with the dictates of modern science. For what is it that, after all, this doctrine implies? Is it not simply that there exists in the world a principle of heredity by which we reproduce the experiences of our ancestors. Modern science declares that it is the mark of a primitive age to affirm that all the sorrows of life are the result of personal wrong-doing. It declares that to call a man wicked because his lot has been cast in unpleasant places, is to resort to a mode of thinking which belongs to an age of infancy. Now this is precisely the view which has been anticipated in the Jewish Scriptures. The Bible reveals that it is not written from the standpoint of a primitive age, or from the altitude of a period of infancy, by distinctly repudiating that doctrine which modern science repudiates. It declares that so far are the sufferings of life from being the necessary marks of a personal degeneracy, that these sufferings may in a multitude of cases be actually referred to a totally different principle. It affirms that there is a law in the universe by which the sins of the fathers may have their penalties postponed to the second or third generation, and visited upon those who have not committed them. It is open for every man to discuss the justice of such an arrangement, but it is not open for him to deny its naturalness. Here, if anywhere, the God of the Bible is at one with that principle of modern science which is called Nature. In both cases there is recognised the fact that there may be a retribution where strictly speaking there is no penalty; that the pain of a violated law may descend upon those who have not violated it; and that the medium through which it descends is a principle which connects the fathers with the children—a principle of heredity.

It is for a similar reason that the Old Testament Scriptures have drawn a sharp distinction between an act of divine forgiveness and the remission of a divine penalty. We allude specially to the narrative of the prophet Nathan's meeting with King David (2 Samuel xii. 13, 14). The point to be observed here is, that there is extended to David by the prophet a full and free forgiveness, "The Lord hath put away thy sin." His crime against Uriah is cancelled, so to speak, from the divine remembrance, his iniquity is blotted out, his sin is covered. One would imagine that, under these circumstances, the matter would have an end; that the sin being covered by God would not be allowed to draw after it its natural penal consequences. This, however, is not the case. The sin is blotted out, but the consequences of the sin are allowed to remain. The king is forgiven, but he is expressly told that notwithstanding this forgiveness he will be obliged to bear that punishment which has resulted from his violation of divine law. The natural sequence which connects an act of crime with a bitter experience is not to be interrupted, even though the penitent has been received into favour; the union of sin and suffering is still to continue unbroken, and the penalty is to be borne, even after the pardon has come. Now, we say, this distinction drawn by the Bible between an act of divine forgiveness and the remission of a divine penalty is a very significant and a very scientific one. It shows that in the mind of the Jew the idea of retribution was distinguished from the idea of personal punishment. David's personal punishment may be said to have been remitted; he was no longer asked to receive the penalty of an injured law as a mandate addressed to his *conscience*, he was already a forgiven man. None the less was he still a subject of retribution; he had violated a law of Nature, and the violated law avenged itself. The retribution which he was called to undergo was precisely that kind of retribution which is allowed by the modern man of science to belong to the system of the universe—a retribution which, because it lay in the order of things, could not be cancelled even by an act of divine forgiveness.

Let us now try to transfer the language of the psalmist into the language of the scientist. Let us see whether the words of this first psalm have become obsolete to the modern view of the universe.

To test this point let us substitute for the Jewish word God the scientific word Nature, and let us apply to the latter those words which the psalmist applied to the former. Let us see, in short, whether the psalm of David is capable of being made a veritable psalm of science! Let us suppose that it read thus: "Blessed is the man that walketh not in the counsel of the unnatural, nor standeth in the way of those who transgress the law of Nature, nor sitteth in the seat of those who scoff at the law of Nature; but whose delight is in Nature's law, and who meditates on that law day and night. He shall be like a tree planted by the rivers of water, that bringeth forth his fruit in his season; his leaf also shall not wither; and whatsoever he doeth shall prosper. The unnatural are not so; but they are like unto the chaff which the wind driveth away." The question is, Would such a psalm be an anachronism in the ear of modern science? Would it seem contrary to the truth which modern science is commissioned to teach? The last clause would certainly be accepted unqualifiedly. The modern scientist would subscribe with all his heart to the truth of the doctrine "the unnatural are not so; but they are like unto the chaff which the wind driveth away." To the man of science the greatest sin in the universe is to set one's self in opposition to the *law* of the universe—in other words, to be unnatural. It is a distinct part of his creed that the man who runs counter to Nature is thereby shortening his days, is putting himself out of harmony with those forces of life which naturally conduce to the survival of the organism. Accordingly, the man of science would freely accede to the position that the systematic transgressor and scorner of the law of Nature is by his own act doomed to perish, and is liable to be driven away by every wind that blows: he would unreservedly admit the negative side of the psalmist's doctrine—that he who violates Nature's law is the man who is not blessed.

But the difficulty our modern scientist would experience would be in accepting the positive side of the psalmist's doctrine. That the transgressor of Nature is unblessed, he would not only readily grant, but strenuously maintain. The case will be otherwise, however, when he is asked to put his imprimatur to the belief that the man who *keeps* the law of Nature shall be like a tree planted by the rivers of water, with abundance of fruit, and unfadingness of leaf, and undimishedness of prosperity. He will naturally ask where there is to be found in the universe any example of such prosperity. He will challenge the religious world to produce any single instance of a man whose life exhibits an unbroken round of successes and a perpetual fadelessness of joy. He will point to the representatives of the highest Christian life as examples of the fact that the promise of the psalmist is not fulfilled. Nor is it possible to refute such a challenge on the part of the scientist. There has not yet appeared in this world an illustration of that perfect beatitude which has been sketched by the pen of the psalmist of Israel. There has not yet been seen amongst the sons of men that life of which it can be said that whatsoever he hath done has prospered. The greatest saint has frequently, from a worldly point of view, been less favoured than the greatest sinner, and the storms which have encountered the man of God have not seldom left untouched the life of the ungodly.

Is, then, the utterance of the psalmist unscientific? Is his promise contradicted by the facts of experience? Assuredly not; the most that can be said is that experience has not yet realised it. For, let us consider how the case stands. It is quite true that we have never seen the altogether prosperous man; but have we ever seen the man who has fulfilled that condition which the psalmist has prescribed as the road to absolute prosperity? We have not met in our experience with the life which has been successful in all its ways and fadeless in all its joys; but have we ever met with that life which has in all its ways walked unerringly in the counsels of Nature, and meditated on its law day and night? None would maintain more strenuously than the psalmist that we have not. The whole burden of his songs is this: "There is none righteous, no, not one." His perfect man is by his own admission an ideal man. He does not exist in the actual life of this world; he exists as yet only in the anticipations of the heart. Let us suppose that the psalmist's anticipation were to be actually realised; let us suppose that once in human history there were to be seen in the natural man what Christians see in the Divine Man—a perfect human life; even then we could not expect to see a life of absolute prosperity. The life of the Divine Man Himself is professedly the life of a man of sorrows. It is so by reason of the sin of others, and by reason of the fact that the lives of others are inextricably bound up with our own. It is not enough for my prosperity that personally I should be able to walk in the perfect law of Nature. I have come into a world in which others are daily and hourly transgressing that law; and it is inevitable that the consequences of their transgression should fall upon me. If I am pure and they are impure, it is all the more inevitable; it is the verdict of universal experience that the best men suffer soonest from the sins of the worst. Their suffering is not to them a penalty, but it is none the less a retribution; it is not a personal vengeance, yet it is the vindication of an outraged law.

We arrive, then, at this conclusion: the connection drawn by the psalmist between a life of purity and a life of prosperity is not a thought which stamps his writings with the mark of a primitive age. It is not an idea which has been exploded by the course of modern research. On the contrary, the course of modern research, so far as it has yet gone, has been thoroughly on the lines of the psalmist's position. Modern science, like ancient Judaism, strenuously asserts that there is the most intimate connection between a violation of Nature's law and the experience of pain; on the negative side of the question they are already at one. If they are not yet at one on the positive side, it is not because the Jewish creed is an anachronism, but because the condition prefigured by that creed has not yet been fulfilled. We have never seen in actual experience the man of perfect blessedness, because we have never seen in actual experience the man of perfect life. To meet with the perfectly blessed man, we would require to meet not only with the man perfectly holy, but with the man perfectly intellectual. The law of Nature is not simply the law of the Decalogue; it is the law of the universe itself—the condition according to which things alone can live. To keep the requirements of Nature a man would need not merely the harmlessness of the dove, but the wisdom of the serpent. He would require to avoid not alone those acts of violence involved in breaking the Ten Commandments, but those acts of imprudence or of ignorance involved in a breach of the principle of gravitation, or in a violation of the law of political economy. Every rule which conduces to the maintenance of life is, scientifically speaking, a law of Nature; religiously speaking, a law of God. And he who would inherit the promise of the psalmist must perfectly conform to the length and the breadth of that law. To be a perfect man is to be in perfect harmony with one's environment, to find an adequate response from every side of the universe. That stage of happy consummation has not yet been reached in experience, and therefore has not yet been tabulated in the records of physical science. But science is already warranted to say that the thought of the psalmist is ideally true. It is already prepared to confess that if ever this world shall produce a being with modes of mind fitted to all the modes of Nature, that being shall in perfect communion with Nature enjoy the perfect blessedness of which the psalmist sings. And the reason why science is prepared to make this concession is the testimony of its own observation, that wherever a mode of mind is unsuited to a mode of Nature, there is ever experienced by that mind a sense of unrest, of sorrow, or of pain. It has been proved to the satisfaction of science that all the pain in this world is the result of non-adaptation, that all the unrest in this world flows from an absence of congruity between the subject and the object. It has been shown with ever-increasing power that just in proportion as the adaptation grows, there grows the sense of human blessedness. The march of civilisation is, by the verdict of modern science, a march nearer to the realisation of that goal, and it is so because, in the view of modern science, that which men call the march of civilisation is an ever-increasing congruity between the modes of the human mind and the modes of universal nature. Are we not here brought very near to the psalmist's own discovery: "In Thy presence is fulness of joy; at Thy right hand there are pleasures for evermore"? He looks for the advent of a time of perfect blessedness, and he sees it in the coming of that age when, to use scientific language, there shall be a complete congruity between the organism and the power called Nature. To be in full communion with Nature, to be at the right hand of Nature, to be adapted on every side of one's being to the presence of that universal law which is the law of Nature, is, alike in the view of the scientist as in the view of the psalmist, the goal of perfect happiness, the consummation towards which every soul should tend. And, alike in the view of the scientist as in the view of the psalmist, there is recognised the truth of the great retributive principle that nearness to that goal is approximation to life, and that distance from it is approximation to death. Both are at one in acceptance of the theory that the man who shall walk according to the law of Nature shall be like a tree planted by the rivers of water, whose leaf shall not fade, and whose fruit shall appear in its season.

CHAPTER XI.

THE PSALMIST'S VIEW OF SIN.

PSALM li. 1-12.

IN the previous chapter we arrived from the standpoint of science at a conclusion analogous to, if not identical with, the conviction of the religious sentiment. We found that the source of all blessedness is to be in uninterrupted harmony with Nature, which in the language of religion is to say—in unbroken communion with God. We found that as a matter of scientific experiment it was admitted and demonstrated that the secret of dispeace, of sorrow, of pain, is always to be traced to some defect in the harmony of the organism with its environment; which again, in religious language, is to say—that the secret of worldly unrest is defective communion with God. We found by the admission of science that when the organism is not in harmony with its environment it transgresses a law of Nature, and that by reason of its transgressing this law of Nature it becomes liable to retribution. The transgression of a law of Nature, therefore, is in the language of of science synonymous with what in the speech of religion is known by the name of sin. In a well-known Christian formula sin is defined to be "any want of conformity unto or transgression of the law of God." Substitute the word Nature for God, and you may transfer the definition of the Westminster Catechism into the creed of modern science. The doctrine of modern science recognises the fact that all the retributions of Nature flow either from the absence of conformity or from the presence of hostility between the organism and its environment. Sometimes an organism is found to be incapable of subsisting in a particular soil or climate; in this case the death of the organism is the retributive result of that violation of Nature's law which comes from want of *conformity*. It has met with retribution, not by doing the things which it ought not to have done, but by leaving undone the things which it ought to have done. At other times, again, we find an organism indulging in a life of active excesses, wasting its substance in riotous living, and imperilling by its riotousness the substance of others. The result of such a life is not long delayed, and is speedily made manifest; the end of such things is death. Yet in this case the death has proceeded from an opposite form of the violation of Nature's law. It has no longer come from a want of conformity to the law, but from a transgression of the law; no longer from leaving undone the things which should have been performed, but from doing those things which ought not to have been performed. The world of science thus reveals a twofold method of violating the law of Nature, exactly analogous to that which constitutes the twofold division of the well-known religious formula.

There are some sins to which we are accustomed to apply the word unnatural. We commonly attribute the term to those manifestations of evil which reveal a bad feeling between the relationships of life. If a son refuses to support his parent, we say his conduct is unnatural. This is simply in scientific language to say that he is not in harmony with that part of his environment which is most closely connected with himself. But the Bible would apply the word unnatural to all forms of sin without exception. It would agree with common experience, that to disregard the relationships of life is an act contrary to nature; but it would on the other hand maintain that the relationships of life are much wider in their scope than is popularly supposed. It is unnatural that a son should refuse to support the declining years of his parent; but on Biblical principles it is equally unnatural that a man should attempt to injure the interests of his fellow-man. And the reason is, that on Biblical principles the family relationship is one which extends to all the

members of the human race. Judaism is commonly
looked upon as the most exclusive of all religions—
as a faith which recognised no brotherhood outside
the circle of its own nationality. From a certain
point of view this is true, but it is not the whole
truth. From the very dawn of its history the
Hebrew race was impregnated with the belief that
its destiny was cosmopolitan, that its mission was to
all mankind. "In thee shall all families of the
earth be blessed," are the words in which the destiny of the nation is revealed; and through all its
checkered history it never for a moment lost sight of
that golden thread which bound its fate to the fate
of other lands. That it looked upon itself as a peculiar people, set apart from the rest of mankind, is
undeniably true; but it held itself to be set apart
only in order that it might be a light-bearer to the
surrounding darkness. It contemplated the time
when all nations would be gathered within its own
empire; but it contemplated that time only because
it saw in its own empire the reign of the King of
kings. It believed itself to be the repository of
divine revelation; but at the same time it was
deeply conscious that it held that revelation only
in trust for humanity. Accordingly, the law of
Judaism was a law of universal brotherhood—an
assertion of the principle that all the families of
the earth were ideally and prospectively the branches
of one family. To sin against a fellow-man, to vio-

late the interests of one's neighbour, was viewed as in the strictest sense an unnatural deed. It was an act contrary to God, because it was an act contrary to nature. It was a violation of that principle of family relationship which God had established in the world, and which He had made coextensive with the world; it broke the harmony of that divine household which already in the divine thought comprehended all the sons of men.

Now let it be observed that in the psalm which we have taken as the representative of the Judaic view of sin, extreme stress is laid upon the fact that it is something unnatural, something contrary to the ideal order of things. This is clearly brought out in the words of verse 10: "Create in me a clean heart, O God; and renew a right spirit within me." It is implied in these words that the heart and spirit of man are now in an unnatural condition; that in order to put them into harmony with the life of nature they require to be renewed and re-created. We are so familiar with the words that we are apt to become oblivious to the fact that they cover a great paradox, that they express a sentiment diametrically opposite to the view commonly entertained. The view commonly entertained is that the regeneration from sin is something which lifts man into the region of the transcendental and supernatural. The view of the psalmist is that the state of sin is itself something opposed to the course of nature, and that the act of regeneration, so far from being a transference into the supernatural, is in reality a restoration into the order of the universe. The Bible is commonly thought to derive its peculiar distinction from the fact that it points man to a life which is miraculous and abnormal. The Bible itself makes a totally different claim to pre-eminence. The revelation which it professes to send makes its appeal to the heart of man, not on the ground that it is miraculous and abnormal, but on the ground that the present state of things is miraculous and abnormal. It bases its claim to acceptance on the fact that the present condition of things is unnatural, that the course of nature has deviated from its original orbit, and thereby become unfit for its environment. It professes to restore the lost balance of the universe, to bring back the course of nature into its original orbit, and to re-establish the broken harmony between the forms of organic life and the objects which were designed to minister to them.

If the view of the Bible be accepted, the revelation which it brings, so far from being unscientific, is really a revelation of the true road to a scientific position. In the view of the Bible man is not now in a scientific position; he is in a position contrary to nature. The nearest approach to supernaturalism, according to this conception, is to be found in the present life of sin. The life of sin is supernatural in respect of being outside the order of nature. It is rather a remarkable circumstance how frequently this thought appears in the songs of the psalmist. In Ps. xiv. 3, it is said of transgressors, "they are all gone aside;" in Ps. liii. 3, it is written, "every one of them is gone back." The going aside and the going back mark a separation from the ordinary and natural track; they imply that the subjects of them have fallen into an unscientific position, into a course deviating from the course of nature. The same thought appears with even greater prominence in Ps. i. 6: "The Lord knoweth the way of the righteous: but the way of the ungodly shall perish." The idea is, that the way of transgressors is so pathless that it is unknown even to God, that it cannot be traced even by the eye of Omniscience. In this bold paradox the psalmist figures the thought that sin is something out of the common way, something unnatural and abnormal, something miraculous and monstrous. To call it supernatural would convey a wrong impression, because we commonly limit the word supernatural to the things which are above nature; but if there were such a word in English as *infra*natural, it would clearly express the idea of the Bible and of the psalmist. Sin is something *below* nature. It is a life of disorder existing in the midst of order. Its abnormal character is recognised by the fact that there is really a divine order in the universe to which it refuses to conform. Regeneration, instead of being a miraculous act, is professedly an act which dissipates the miracle, which dispels the abnormality. The heart is now existing in a corrupt state: it is unclean, and therefore it is unnatural; regeneration's work is to create a *clean* heart, to restore the natural function of the organism. The spirit is now existing in an unsteadfast state; the phrase "a right spirit" literally means a steadfast spirit. The idea is that the life of sin deprives man of sufficient strength to carry out the law of nature; he cannot remain fixed in that principle of action which alone leads to self-preservation. Regeneration's work is to "renew a steadfast spirit," to restore that equilibrium or mental balance which shall enable a man to persevere in the true course of nature. The act of redemption as contemplated by the Bible is an act by which the human soul is to be brought from a life which contradicts nature into union with a life which is natural and normal.

In strict harmony with this conception are the words of this fifty-first psalm, "Against Thee, Thee only, have I sinned, and done this evil in Thy sight." The psalmist is popularly thought to mean that he chiefly abhorred his act, not because it was committed against society, but because it was committed against a private individual. The meaning of the passage, in our opinion, is exactly the reverse. The psalmist wishes to say that his horror of sin originates in the fact that it is not merely a violation of private right, but a violation of natural order. When he says, "Against Thee, Thee only, have I sinned," he is certainly addressing a personal Being. But we must remember that although the God of the Old Testament was a Person, He was also more than a Person; He was before all things a personal Lawgiver. The God against whom the psalmist confesses to have sinned is pre-eminently and distinctively the God of order. He is the Being who has given law to the universe, and on whose law men ought to meditate day and night. The psalmist condemns himself because he has outraged the universal order, because he has come into collision with the eternal course of things, because he has committed a deed which has violated that principle of justice on which the pillars of the universe are based. However much he deplores the suffering he may have caused to a fellow-man, however much he regrets the loss he may have inflicted on a private individual, the main source of his remorse lies in this, that his deed has broken the harmony of the universe, and separated between himself and the God of order.

Perhaps, however, it may be thought that what renders the conception of the psalmist unscientific is just that word which we have used in the last sentence—remorse. The scientific spirit of our age will be ready to grant the existence of sin in the sense in which we have here defined it; but the sense in which we have here defined it does not necessarily include the conception of *guilt*. Every violation of nature's law involves retribution; but every violation of nature's law does not involve guilt, or that sense of guilt which we call remorse. If I violate the law of gravitation I have violated a law of God as much as if I had broken the Decalogue; but I may violate the law of gravitation involuntarily, and as the result of concurring circumstances; in this case I am equally the subject of retribution, but I am not the subject of guilt. Now the tendency of modern science is to hold that every act of sin is produced analogously to the involuntary violation of a law of gravity. Modern science proposes to apply to the existence of sin that great doctrine by which it professes to explain all other things—the doctrine of evolution. It tells us that sin, however disorderly it may be, and however unharmonious with the ideal symmetry of the universe, is yet bequeathed from sire to son in an unbroken sequence of heredity, transmitted from generation to generation through a process over which no single generation has any power. Science therefore looks back with an eye of something like pity on the lives of those devotees who wept over their shortcomings. It regards the remorse of the penitent as a phase of mind which belongs to an age that is gone by. It thinks that it was very natural for prophets and psalmists to torment themselves with the memory of the evils they had done, but that had they lived in the nineteenth century they would have found a solace to their sorrow. The doctrine of evolution would have taught them that their tears were thrown away, that they were really blaming themselves for deeds which could not have been averted, and that the sin which they so much deplored was an evil precisely analogous to those other ills which flesh is heir to.

Now it is rather a remarkable circumstance that the very psalm in which the idea of guilt is most prominent is also that psalm which comes nearest to the modern scientific view of sin. No evolutionist of the nineteenth century could have more strongly expressed his belief in the hereditary nature of moral evil than does this old psalmist of Israel. He says in verse 5, "Behold, in iniquity I was brought forth; and in sin did my mother conceive me." No words could more strongly convey his conviction that moral evil shares the hereditary character of every other evil. About evolution in the abstract he knows nothing; he knows only matters of fact. But amongst these matters of fact he recognises the truth that qualities are transmitted. He recognises this truth at the very time when his whole soul is possessed with the thought of his own personal demerit. There is not in the whole psalter, there is not in all literature, a more earnest sense of personal demerit than breathes in this fifty-first psalm. From beginning to end it is pervaded, permeated, inspired by the burden of human guilt. And yet at the very moment in which the psalmist feels his sin as the act of a solitary individual, he is perfectly conscious, and he gives expression to the consciousness, that he is not a solitary individual, that he is not the originator of his own sin, that he is not wholly responsible for all the evil that exists within him. The evil that exists within him had its origin in the lives of his ancestors, and was transmitted to him by the course of natural generation. The psalmist, therefore, is not an object for modern pity, not a target for scientific patronage. He is thoroughly conversant with the fact with which modern science is conversant. He is fully aware that there exists in the world a principle of heredity, and that from the earthly side it is possible on that principle to account for the existence of moral evil in any single soul. We must seek elsewhere for an explanation of the psalmist's bitter cry than in the complacent theory that the nineteenth century has entered on a stage of higher development.

Let us look now at the other side of the picture. We have seen that in the mind of the psalmist the sense of heredity could exist side by side with the sense of guilt. Do we find that in the mind of the scientist the sense of heredity has expelled the sense of guilt? The psalmist has anticipated the scientist in recognising the hereditary descent of sin; has the scientist outgrown the psalmist by outliving the individual sense of guilt? Is it not a matter of common experience that the sense of guilt, so far from being weakened by the advances of civilisation and culture, owes its strongest development to the development of the human mind. The ages of science are claimed by the scientific man as preeminently the ages of morality, the ages in which the principles of life and conduct are to take the place of the principles of metaphysics and philosophy. The man of science believes that sin comes by heredity; he believes also that disease comes by heredity. Yet the sense of sin gives him quite a different impression from that which he experiences from a sensation of hereditary weakness. Let us suppose that a man of science is a prey to that disease which is admitted to run in families—consumption. He is in that case subject at one and the same time to two forms of disease—one physical, and the other moral,—the disease called consumption and the disease called sin. Both of these maladies have one feature in common; each of them is derived from heredity. The scientific man is perfectly aware that he can trace his moral weakness to his father as clearly as he can trace to him his physical weakness. Yet the sense of his moral weakness involves a feeling of pain which is altogether absent from the sense of his physical weakness—that feeling of pain which we call the burden of guilt. He pities himself because he is a prey to consumption; he blames himself because he has been guilty of sin. How are we to account for this difference? Both come by hereditary descent; why should only one of them convey the feeling of guilt? Theological prejudice will not account for it. We are imagining a case from which the element of religion is altogether excluded. We are quite willing to postulate the hypothesis that our scientific man is an atheist; it will make no difference to the present argument. Be he atheist or theist, he will as a human being, and as long as he retains a human heart, experience a sense of remorse for any wrong action he has done to a fellow-man, and will experience it quite irrespective of the fact that he can trace his wrong action to a principle of heredity.

We anticipate here the answer which would probably be given by the scientific man himself. He would tell us that there is no difficulty whatever in explaining why the idea of guilt, which is absent from the physical weakness, attaches itself to the moral weakness. He would point to the fact that the moral weakness has for generations and centuries been a subject of retribution. He would tell us that the disease called sin has been visited with penalties from time immemorial, that it has been punished by

Church and State, that it has involved its perpetrator in countless pains and dangers. He would tell us that if the disease called consumption had been for generations and centuries subjected to the same penalties it would by this time have suggested to the man afflicted with it the same idea of guilt. He would tell us that our impressions for the most part come from the manner in which our ideas have been associated, that deeds which have been linked with pain become inevitably repulsive to the mind. The moral disease has been for ages associated with the thought of retribution, and therefore it has acquired in the fulness of time an appearance of originality which seems to separate it from the natural course of evolution.

Now, waiving altogether the question whether any circumstances whatsoever could have associated the disease called consumption with the idea of guilt, we confine ourselves here to one point. Whatever be the reason why the idea of guilt is not associated with the disease, that reason is not the absence of retribution. For, as a matter of fact, the notion of retribution is as much present in the disease called consumption as it is in the disease called sin. The man who is subject to consumption is a subject of retribution. Not only is retribution associated with his disease in *idea*, it is associated with it in fact. We have already pointed out that every form of pain is in the strictest sense of the word retributive. We have seen that pain originates in the circumstance that there has somewhere arisen an incongruity between the organism and its environment. It is the struggle of the organism to get back to its original position, to regain that equilibrium and that equanimity which are the inevitable result of harmony between the organism and the things which surround it. Pain is accordingly the protest of a violated law against its violation—in other words, it is retributive. There is no reason whatever why a man who is afflicted with consumption, or with any other form of disease, should not every day of his life associate his own pain with the idea of retribution, with the thought of some penalty exacted as the result of a violated law; yet, however constant such an association may be, however uninterrupted in his mind be the sequence between the idea of disease and the thought of retribution, there will never for a moment arise the slightest impression that he has done anything wrong: by no combination of circumstances, by no possible grouping of associations, will the man in the case supposed ever awake to an imagination that his physical pain involves a sense of moral guilt. Not only will it be impossible for him to conceive such a thought spontaneously, it will be impossible for him to receive it at the suggestion of another; the moment it is presented to him it will be at once and unhesitatingly rejected. We are bound, therefore, to conclude that the explanation offered by science why the moral disease involves a sense of guilt not involved in other diseases, is an explanation which cannot stand. It is refuted by the facts of experience, refuted by the positive method of science itself. It has been proved to demonstration that every disease involves the idea of retribution as clearly as does the disease called sin. The explanation, accordingly, why the disease called sin should alone be accompanied by the sense of guilt, is not here to be found.

Can it be found anywhere? Such is the question which again and again has been asked by the human mind in contemplating the problem of its own contradictions. We are not speaking of the problem called the origin of evil; that is an insoluble puzzle. It is popularly thought that the Bible is distinguished from other books by the refusal to admit its insolubility. A greater delusion was never conceived. The Bible nowhere professes to assign an origin to sin. It professes to indicate a time, or rather to indicate that there *was* a time, when sin began in the human race; but it distinctly rejects the notion that its beginning in the human race was its beginning in the universe. It introduces the mystery of iniquity with the same abruptness with which it introduces the mystery of Godhead. "The serpent was more subtil than any beast of the field." Even if we appended to the narrative of Genesis the later narrative of "angels who kept not their first estate," the Bible would not bring us one step nearer to the ultimate solution of the mystery; for it is at least as hard to explain the origin of evil in the mind of an angel, as to explain the origin of evil in the mind of a man. The Bible, accordingly, nowhere speculates on this subject. The Psalms are full of penitence, but they never diverge from the contemplation of present degeneracy. They are concerned purely with the question *what* sin is—they do not ask *why* it is. The psalmist of Israel follows in the spiritual world the same method of Positivism which the scientist follows in the natural world. He keeps strictly to facts, the facts of his inner experience. He does not ask whence these facts originated; he is content with knowing that they are there. We shall follow on this occasion his example. We shall leave untouched that side of the question which he has passed by. But the point on which we now seek light is not a speculative one; it belongs to the region of Positivism, it is practical, it is experimental. We find two facts within our own experience, both of which were discovered by the psalmist nearly three thousand years ago. We find, on the one hand, that we are the subjects of a moral disease, which has not originated within ourselves, but has come down to us through ancestors; we find, on the other hand, that notwithstanding the fact that this moral disease has not originated within ourselves, we feel, in contemplating it, precisely that sense of personal demerit which we would experience had we been consciously its originators. This is the paradox which we want to explain. Each of the facts is by itself undoubtedly true and perfectly undeniable; each of them seems at the same time incompatible with the existence of the other. Sin is a disease as hereditary as any other malady, and yet, unlike every other malady, the man who is a subject of it is compelled to experience a sense of blame; how are we to account for this? It is independent of all questions regarding the origin of evil, irrespective of all beliefs concerning Adam and the Garden of Eden. It lies at the door of our own being, and it meets us the moment we open the door. It is a mystery which confronts the man of science as surely as it confronted the psalmist of Israel. Is there any possible road by which an escape may be found from this greatest paradox of human nature?

It seems to us that we shall find such an escape suggested in the words of this psalm itself. It will be observed that when it is said, "Create in me a clean heart, O God; and renew a steadfast spirit within me," there is an allusion made to two distinct parts of man's nature: one is called the heart, and the other the spirit. It will be observed, also, that these two sides of man's nature are not spoken of in precisely the same way. The heart is said to be naturally unclean; the spirit is declared to be simply unsteadfast. The heart is therefore represented as by nature in a more hopeless condition than the spirit. It will be observed, finally, that in conformity with this thought, it is clearly suggested by the psalmist that the heart, in order to be purified, requires a more radical work than the spirit. He calls upon God to *create* a clean heart within him; he asks Him simply to *renew* a steadfast spirit. The distinction is not meant to be a merely verbal one, designed to further the parallelism of Hebrew poetry. The heart, in the psalmist's view, is absolutely corrupt, and nothing will avail but absolute regeneration—in other words, the *creating* of a *clean* heart. The spirit, on the other hand, retains the germ of right impulses, if it could only remain constant in their exercise. Accordingly, there is wanted for the spirit something less than absolute regeneration; it will be sufficient to have it so renewed that it will be steadfast in its aspirations, true to itself.

These are the facts of the case as they appear on the page of the psalmist. What is the interpretation of these facts? When the psalmist speaks of a clean heart and a steadfast spirit, he clearly means to distinguish two different sides of human nature. What is the distinction which is here present to his mind? Perhaps it will be best represented by saying that the distinction he designs to draw between the heart and the spirit is tantamount to the difference we desire to describe when we speak of the affections and the will. Strictly speaking, the distinction between the affections and the will is not a just or logical one. When the mind is actuated by any affection towards an object, it is really actuated by a form of will; when the mind is influenced by an act of will, it is really influenced by a form of affection. The distinction, therefore, is not correct in logic, but it may be allowed to pass in popular description. We shall therefore, for the present purpose, adopt this division here as a descriptive equivalent for the *heart* and the *spirit* of the psalmist. What the psalmist means to say is that in moral action the mind is influenced in two ways—by the feelings and by the intellect. It sometimes acts in obedience to the promptings of pleasurable or painful sensation; at others, it refuses to follow any guidance but that of intellectual judgment. In the former case, the psalmist would say that the man has been ruled by the heart; in the latter, he would say that he has been directed by the spirit. The heart and the spirit are therefore both forms of volition, but they are different forms of volition: the heart is the will impelled by feeling, the spirit is the will impelled by judgment.

Let us proceed a step further with the psalmist's analysis. In his view it is clearly implied that in the present state of human nature there is a great difference between the power of choice possessed by the spirit or intellectual will, and the power of choice possessed by the heart or sensitive will. The intellectual will is, in his view, still strong for good; the sensitive will is utterly weak and powerless. The intellectual judgments of the spirit point unerringly towards right; if its steadfastness were equal to its intuition, the spirit would be pure. What renders the spirit impure is the fact that it has not strength enough to indorse its own moral decisions; it exhausts itself in the first effort, it requires to be renewed in order that it may be steadfast. The sensitive affections, on the other hand, are greatly under the dominion of the animal life; they are so enslaved by inferior motives that they are unable, in their present state, to behold the right way, and before they can be made capable of beholding it, they will require to undergo a process of complete metamorphosis, demanding nothing less than a new creation.

It cannot have escaped the reader that this analysis of the psalmist is identical with that analysis of man's moral nature which is given by Immanuel Kant. So far from being an anachronism from the standpoint of modern science, it is almost an exact anticipation of the doctrine of one whom, of all philosophers, modern science has been most disposed to follow. Kant, as is well known, recognised a dualism in human nature. He, like the psalmist, was conscious that the moral actions of man were no longer the result of free choice; but he was equally conscious that there existed in man the belief that he was free. To the German philosopher, as to the Jewish psalmist, there presented itself that ever-recurring problem, why, in one and the same being, two such opposite experiences could possibly dwell? If, in point of fact, man was not free, why did he feel himself to be responsible? if he felt himself to be responsible, why was he not free? It was perfectly clear to Kant that the one state could never have proceeded from the other. The slavery of man's animal nature could not have originated his sense of responsibility; his sense of responsibility could never have given birth to the slavery of his animal nature. In the present state of things Kant could find no bridge between these two experiences, and therefore he was obliged to seek the bridge in a state of things beyond the present. The existence of a sense of responsibility in the midst of actual bondage constituted to Kant the strongest argument for immortality. If there was nothing in man's actual condition that could account for it, it must be accounted for by something outside of man's actual condition. There must be somewhere a supersensuous world, a house not made with hands, eternal in the heavens. In every moral act there is a voice which says to the human soul "thou shalt," "thou shalt not." It speaks with a mandate from which there is no appeal. It gives no reason for its command; its will is the only reason. It utters its law at the very moment when we have resolved to disobey it, at the very moment when we are actually disobeying it. If a man yields to the temptation of taking that which is not his own, the Mount Sinai within him thunders forth, "Thou shalt not!" If a man refuses to go out of his way to help a brother in distress, the Mount Sinai within him proclaims in trumpet-tones, "Thou shalt!" There are often, at one and the same moment, two voices heard in the soul of man—contradictory voices, irreconcilable voices; but voices which speak together. How is such an anomaly to be explained? Kant says that by anything in the present world it cannot be explained. Man cannot be at one and the same moment the maker and the breaker of the law; he cannot simultaneously decide to follow and to reject a certain course of action. There is only one remaining explanation. There must be a portion of man's nature which, although *in* the world, is not *of* the world. The law which says "thou shalt," "thou shalt not," cannot be given by the same being who is already disobeying it. It must have come from above, and it must point to its fulfilment above. It tells us we are free, but in this world we are not free. Our freedom is only an idea, only a thought, only an aspiration; is it to be also only an illusion? It must be so if this life be all. To redeem it from illusion, to account for the fact of its existence at all, we are bound to postulate the existence of a higher life within the soul; a life to which the soul once belonged, and to which the soul shall yet return.

It will be seen how near this modern view of Kant approaches, not only to the sentiment of the psalmist, but to the spirit of that primitive narrative which records the fall of man. It is rather singular that the latest and ripest fruit of philosophy has not substantially transcended the philosophy of the Garden of Eden. Waiving this question, however, let us confine ourselves to the application of this theory to the words of the psalmist. He too has recognised a dualism in the nature of man. He sees a heart which is enslaved, and he beholds a spirit which is free; the former needs to be wholly re-created, the latter requires only to be renewed. Accordingly, the mind of the psalmist is conscious of a double experience, arising from the double side of his nature. On the one hand he feels that the evil within him has come to him by heredity; that he is bound with a chain which he himself did not make. On the other hand he feels himself to be the author of his own iniquity, answerable to his own conscience, responsible for his own actions. A paradox it certainly is; but it is no more a paradox in the writings of the psalmist than in the works of the German philosopher. It is not a contradiction which belongs to the speculations of an infantile age; it is a contradiction which belongs to human nature itself, and which, therefore, must be reproduced in all ages. Let us now see in what light this contradiction stands with reference to the creed of modern science.

The modern doctrine of evolution is at war with the notion that the will is free. The very conception of evolution is the conception of a chain in which each link is rigidly connected with an antecedent link. Every moral act of the spirit of man is recognised in this system as the product of a previous act, as that is of an act earlier still. This is the doctrine which is commonly known by the name Determinism—the doctrine that a man's destiny in the future has already been decided for him in the past; that the acts of his mind can be traced to mechanical causes as surely as the acts of his body, and that what seems the result of a free personality is referable to a long series of causes over which he has had no control. Now, as we have seen, the modern scientist is here not contradicted by the ancient psalmist. The psalmist has also looked out on the nature of man from a mechanical point of view, and he has found that, from a mechanical point of view, the moral acts of each human soul admit of being traced back to an indefinite past. "I was brought forth in iniquity; and in sin did my mother conceive me," are the words in which he expresses his sense that man is not free. It is a bold and uncompromising statement of the influence of heredity in the moral world. He recognises his present iniquity as the result of a mental state which existed within him at the hour of his birth; he recognises it as the result of something which existed in his embryonic state before birth; and, going back further still, he recognises it as the result of something which existed beforehand in the heart of his parent. Language could no more strongly indicate the psalmist's conviction that there is a side of man's moral nature which is explicable on mechanical principles, and on which, therefore, man is not free; the psalmist and the scientist are here at one.

But does the creed of the modern scientist on this subject go no further? It does. Professor Huxley, Professor Tyndall, Mr Herbert Spencer, and all thorough-going evolutionists, agree in holding that man is not free; but they also agree in holding that man believes himself to be free. They recognise the existence of a thing in the intellectual world called consciousness—in the moral world conscience. They admit that this thing is of its kind quite peculiar, and that it gives a quite peculiar testimony. Everything in the world of nature testifies to a mechanical origin; conscience tells the soul that it is free. Such is the important fact which is admitted by the modern evolutionist. He does not indeed admit its validity; he declares conscience to be in this respect subject to a delusion, but he abundantly concedes that its actual testimony is adverse to the mechanical view of man's moral nature.

Now we have no intention here of disputing the position of the scientist that the testimony of conscience to the existence of human freedom is a delusion. Perhaps the theologian, certainly the Calvinistic theologian, would agree with the scientist in this. If the individual soul has no promise or potence of a life higher and larger than the life of its original nature, we should be disposed to say that the testimony of conscience *is* a delusion. As we are not writing a theological treatise, but merely instituting a study in comparative religion, we shall not seek to inquire into this point. We shall accept the statement of the modern scientist that the testimony of conscience as to man's freedom is a delusion. We accept it, however, not as a negative but as a positive statement. We take it as the admission of a real fact. Science confesses that there is in the human soul something which gives a testimony adverse to all the other testimonies of nature on the subject of freedom. Nature says we are bound; conscience says we are free. This testimony of conscience is, of course, to be received as a delusion; but even when this is conceded, it is marvellous enough to revolutionise the mechanical view of evolution.

For, let us ask, Whence comes this delusion in the moral nature of man? What is that process of the mind by which, irrespective of all the mechanical facts of nature, and in direct antagonism to the verdict of these facts, philosopher and peasant alike arrive practically at the conclusion that their will is free? It will be found on examination that the verdict of conscience, however delusory, really rests upon a premiss. It is not simply an imagination; if received as imaginary it must be received as an imagination of reason. The reason why all men in practical life believe their will to be free is the fact that the intellectual choice of the will is invariably in favour of right. The statement may seem a paradox, and in relation to the other facts of human nature a paradox it certainly is, but it is none the less unquestionably true. The intellectual will of man always decides for the right in preference to the wrong. The proof lies in this, that the intellectual will of man always pronounces a wrong action to *be* wrong. At the very moment when a man has determined to pursue a course of sin, at the very moment when he is actually engaged in travelling over that course, at the very moment when he is experiencing the most intense pleasure in the pursuit of his projected wickedness, he confesses to himself that he is doing *wrong*. The confession may not be accompanied by any remorse; the predominance of the animal life within him may have deadened that original sensitiveness which he felt at the commission of evil; but, however deadened he may be, there never comes a time in which he, as a reasonable being, ceases to distinguish between the right and the wrong. Now this may seem a very trivial circumstance; its very commonplaceness makes it appear of little value. In reality, however, it is one of the most important facts in the whole sphere of morals. Why do I say in the act of committing any crime that I am doing *wrong?* Would it be possible for me to say so unless the act had been rejected by some part of my nature? Right and wrong are degrees of comparison; when I distinguish between them I prefer the one to the other. If I follow the wrong course, and still continue to call it wrong, I am still preferring the right with one part of my nature. If a man in the midst of the utmost degradation feels himself to *be* in degradation, his intellectual will has really chosen the upper path; it is only by such an act of choice that he could ever become conscious of his debasement. The drunkard may have become such a slave to his cups that he is unable to conceive life pleasurable without them; but would the drunkard like to see his child inherit the same tendency? The illustration is a pertinent one, because it shows how at one and the same time there is present in the human soul a sense of slavery and an exercise of freedom. The man could not endure a life of sobriety for himself; he could not endure anything else for his son. Here is a dualism—the old dualism that meets us in the psalmist, the modern dualism that appears in the speculations of Kant. We see on one side of human nature the presence of a chain which has so long bound it that it has ceased to be galling; we behold on the other the act of an unfettered will which in the very midst of the chain insists on being free. On the one side, we are confronted by the effects of hereditary transmission, the results of an evolutionary process which seems to have reduced the individual to the dimensions of a piece of mechanism; on the other, we are met by the individual himself refusing to receive the hereditary bias, powerless to shake it off, yet resolute in maintaining that it ought not to be. That resolution is the mystery of human nature, the guarantee to man that he is larger than he seems. It is an act of free choice in the midst of slavery, an admiration of beauty in the midst of a world whose ideal is shapelessness and deformity. It may be a delusion in him to believe that he can ever carry out his choice; it may be a delusion to suppose that he possesses the power to break the iron chain that binds him; but the existence of such a delusion is itself his act of freedom; the presence of such a fancy is itself the wondrous fact that declares him to be a man.

Let us now try for a moment to throw ourselves back into the position of the psalmist. He has committed, we shall say, some great act of sin. The popular notion, as is well known, is that this psalm was not dictated by any mere horror of sin in the abstract, but was the product of David's anguish for the commission of a special deed of wrong—the murder of Uriah. For our present purpose it matters little whether the deed of the psalmist has or has not been rightly identified. It is enough to say that he is conscious in his own mind of having performed some glaring act of transgression. The consciousness fills him with pain. He feels himself to be a degraded being, unclean in the sight of Heaven, an outcast from the assembly of the just. He looks into his own conscience, and he beholds there a mirror of himself which startles him. He shrinks back from the image in dismay, and there rises in his heart the conviction that if even he, a poor sinful being, recoils from the sight of sin, the recoil of Divine Purity must be infinitely greater. In his agony of soul he prepares to pour forth his penitence, to supplicate for mercy, to pray for cleansing. Let us now suppose, however, that before entering on this supplication, there came into his mind a new thought. Imagine that he had begun to reason thus: After all, am I not tormenting myself unduly? I am vexing my soul with the idea that I have committed a deed of sin; ought I not to remember that I did not originate my own sin? Should I not bear in mind that "I was brought forth in iniquity, and in sin did my mother conceive me"? If my sin has been hereditary, is it not a delusion in me to imagine that I am blameworthy? This conscience of mine has been deceiving me all along; it has been telling me that I am free. Ought I not to hold its testimony as of no value, seeing it is a testimony which stands opposed to the verdict of all the other facts of human nature?

Now it is quite possible, nay, we should think it is almost certain, that such a thought did pass through the mind of the writer of this psalm. He feels, on the one hand, that he was brought forth in sin; he feels, on the other, that his sin is so blameworthy as to call forth his bitter cry for mercy. It is more than probable that at one period of his reflections the former sentiment presented itself as a solace to the latter, and that the knowledge of his inherited tendency to evil contributed to dull his pain. It is quite certain, however, that this dulling of remorse, if it ever existed, was a merely temporary thing, and that the mental pain gained ultimately a triumphant victory over the momentary solace. The question is, why? If the sense of guilt seemed to be contradicted by the testimony of heredity, why did the psalmist, conceding as he did the truth of heredity, not dismiss the sense of guilt? It was because to him the majesty of the sense of guilt lay in the very fact that it was inexplicable. Heredity could not explain it; heredity seemed to explain it away, to deny its right to existence. Everything in nature pointed to the conclusion that the human soul was not free; the whole order of evolution said to the psalmist, "Thou wert brought forth in iniquity; how then canst thou help thy sin?" But to him the sense of guilt was authoritative, just because it could not be explained. The majesty of the moral law within him was the fact that it thundered from an invisible centre, that it spoke in contradiction of and in defiance of the whole order of mere mechanical evolution. In spite of the power of heredity, in spite of the admitted strength of evolutionary descent, in spite of the concession that he had really been brought forth in iniquity and derived his sin from parental inheritance, the moral law declared that he was a free man, a responsible being, a self-possessing human soul. Whence could the moral law have derived so original a message? Everything within him spoke of his slavery; this one solitary voice proclaimed him to be free. Whence could such a voice have proceeded? It could not be the utterance of mechanical nature, for mechanical nature speaks only one language—the language of necessity. It could not be the product of a materialistic evolution, for materialistic evolution is by definition the very negation of freedom, the denial of the possibility of being free. There was only one remaining supposition:—the voice must come from above. Incapable of being traced to any earthly conditions, at variance in its message with all the voices of surrounding nature, it must have descended from a height beyond the earthly, it must have come from a life higher than the physical. And so the psalmist uncovered his head before this mysterious, this inexplicable mandate; bowed down to it just on account of its mystery, just by reason of its inexplicableness. He believed in the sense of heredity, but he found nothing supernatural about it; he could account for it by the principles of mechanical nature. But he could not account for a voice which in the midst of his prison-house told him he was free; he could not explain a message which in the midst of surrounding materialism commanded him to act as a responsible soul. He was compelled to receive it as a proof that beyond the walls of the prison-house there were fields of illimitable liberty, as a testimony that in the midst of material nature there existed the presence of a Life that was eternal, immortal, and invisible. The psalmist's sense of guilt was his sense of immortality, and his sense of the presence of that God which to him was synonymous with immortality. He bowed down before the law that told him he was guilty, because he recognised in that law a voice, not only above the noise of many waters, but above all the voices of all material things: it was to him omnipotent, because it was to him supernatural.

And here we are naturally brought to that which has often appeared the most obscure feature in the life of ancient Israel—its hope for the future. We find that nation in a very peculiar position in regard to its spiritual creed. On the one hand there are few direct statements of its belief in a life beyond the grave; on the other hand there is found pervading every page of its history an intense, an almost overwhelming, sense of sin. One feels involuntarily and instinctively that the presence of the latter element more than compensates for the absence of the former. Why had the ancient Israelite this overwhelming sense of sin? If he believed in no life beyond the present life, if there existed in his heart no hope of aught beyond the passing day and hour, why was it to him a matter of so much concern that he had sinned and come short of perfection? The psalmist himself would have asked, why? Nothing was to him more clear than the supernatural character of his own sense of guilt. He knew that it never came from beneath, that it could never be accounted for by anything below. And just because he looked in vain for its origin in earthly things, he felt that its origin must be divine. In modern times our sense of guilt is derived from our belief in immortality; the psalmist's belief in immortality was derived from his sense of guilt. *We* begin by thinking of the future state, and then go on to consider our preparedness for that state; *he* began by considering his standard of moral perfection, and thence he concluded that there must be a state beyond. He was brought forth in iniquity, and he inherited his sin as he inherited other possessions; but he felt in the sense of sin what he experienced in the sense of no other possession—an agony of remorse. That remorse came to him as a message from above, just because he could not explain it from below. It was not to be accounted for by the things which were seen and temporal, it was not to be traced to the fleeting and perishable shows of time. Was it not therefore certain that there must be a life behind the seen and temporal, that there must be a principle of being from which all the elements of fleetingness and perishableness were absent? The law which said "Thou shalt not," came not from the changeful and the mutable; must there not be, in order to explain its existence, a region where there is no longer any change or mutation, but where the majesty of moral law abides in eternal strength? Such is the hope of Judaism, a hope which grows out of its very sense of degradation. We have seen that its sense of degradation has not to modern science become an anachronism; we must now go on to see whether the hope which has grown out of it is also susceptible of being scientifically preserved.

T

CHAPTER XII.

THE PSALMIST'S PRINCIPLE OF CONSERVATION.

Psalm lxxiii. 23-28.

THERE are certain phrases in literature which may be said to belong distinctively to modern times, specially to the times of modern science. Most prominent among these are the expressions, "correlation of forces," "principle of conservation," and "principle of continuity." The phrases have really all the same meaning, and denote one scientific fact. Modern science, like ancient philosophy and medieval theology, has been in search of, and professes to have found, a life which abides amid the changeful, a force which remains amid the transient, a principle which continues amid the fleeting and the perishable. It expresses this thought in various ways, but they all amount to the same thing. When it desires to indicate that all the forces of nature are really forms of one and the same force, it uses the phrase "correlation of forces." When it seeks to explain how in the various transmutations of nature there has been no real loss of energy, it employs the expression "principle of conservation." Finally, when it wishes to convey its impression that there is no blank in the universe, but that every form of life and matter is rigidly linked to an antecedent form, it clothes that thought in the statement that there exists in nature a "principle of continuity."

We have said that in the search for this principle modern science has been at one both with ancient philosophy and with medieval theology. We might have said that it has been at one with the whole human race in every age. Modern science is not distinguished from popular life by its search for a principle of continuity. All human life has been distinguished from other life precisely by this search. We find the earliest traces of it in the old Hebrew narrative of the Tower of Babel. Whatever physical explanation may be given of that narrative, its metaphysical explanation is not far to seek. The men of that ancient time wanted something which would be their memorial for all time—something which would prevent their name from perishing, and constitute their immortality through all generations. It was the same instinct, perhaps, which prompted the ancient Egyptians to rear those colossal pyramids which have been the admiration of every age; it was the desire to see perpetuated in time their ideal of national greatness. It is through an analogous impulse that the Chinese empire has sought to establish an almost indefinite antiquity reaching back into the mists of the remotest past; its aim has been to prove its claim to that attribute which it looks upon as the highest glory of a kingdom—the attribute of changelessness. As we pass down to more modern times, we find the minds of men permeated by the same idea—the desire to discover a principle of conservation. What is the origin of that art called alchemy but the attempt to meet, amid the fleeting and the changeable, with a substance which shall be permanent and enduring? What is the search for the philosopher's stone but the endeavour to find a common element in all the various elements of nature, a single force into which all other forces may be correlated? What is the search for the elixir of life but the attempt to discover an abiding vital principle binding together the perishable vital forms, a something which continues unimpaired in the midst of all its fleeting manifestations? The pursuit which has been instituted by modern science is thus no novelty; it is but a continuation of that study which has occupied the mind and heart of humanity during all the ages of its being — the effort to solve the problem of the permanent source of things. It is but seeking in a new form an answer to the very ancient question, What is that which abides, amid the things which pass away?

In speaking of this tendency of modern science, you will distinguish between the principle of conservation and that principle of survival which we considered in a previous chapter. The principle of survival is that by which one form *outlives* another; the principle of conservation is that by which one form persists *through* another. The survival of the fittest means the power of those organisms which are best adapted to their environment to outlast those organisms which are least adapted. The principle of conservation means the power of one force or substance to exist unimpaired through the manifestations of a multitude of forces. Conservation, strictly speaking, means more than survival. Survival does not imply more than endurance after others die; conservation implies the power to keep others alive. It is not merely a principle of immortality, it is a principle of immortalising. It is really conservation, and not simply survival, that humanity has all along been seeking. It is this which the modern scientist has sought in his correlation of forces. It is this which the medieval alchemist has sought in his transmutation of metals. It is this which the believers in the philosopher's stone and the elixir of life have sought—not only a power to be rich, and a power to live for ever, but a power to *make* rich, and a power to make immortal.

Now the Jewish nation has been no exception to the common rule; it too has followed the search of universal humanity for a permanent source of things. Its whole religion, its whole philosophy, has been based upon the belief that amidst the forms which pass away there is something which remaineth, that amidst the things which wax old like a garment there is one which is ever the same. As the representative of this search of Judaism, we have taken the concluding verses of the seventy-third psalm. The subject of these verses may be said to be the changeless in the mutable. The psalmist, in the previous verses, has been recording a bitter experience through which he has passed. His spiritual life had undergone a process analogous to what, in the scientific world, would be called a dissipation of energy. The first freshness of his faith had been lost, the original fervour of his piety had been cooled. He had looked out upon the world as it actually was, and had begun to feel that there was a seeming incongruity between the divine promise and the existing state of things. The righteous had received a pledge of God's sustenance, and it appeared as if that sustenance were given to the wicked. The holy men of the earth had been promised the wealth of the land, and it seemed as if that wealth had been reserved for the unholy. In the contemplation of these facts the psalmist himself had become unholy. The force of his spiritual life had been dissipated, the strength of his animal life had increased. He expresses his conviction of this decline in very strong terms in verse 22—"So foolish was I, and ignorant: I was as a beast before Thee." The thought manifestly is that the spiritual life within him had been undergoing a process of death, and that the animal life which had once been repressed by the spirit had come into fresh power. At length, however, a change had dawned. The temporary decline of faith had been arrested, and the spiritual life had bounded back to its original fervency. The turning-point was marked by the psalmist's discovery of his own degradation, by his recognition of the comparative weakness of his life under the eclipse of faith, "I was as a beast before Thee." But now he makes a discovery more potent still, and carrying a more far-reaching conclusion. He finds that even in his process of death the principle of divine life had never for a moment been absent from him, that even in the deepest decline of his spiritual being there had been an unbroken union between God and his soul. This is really the thought which breaks forth in the words of verse 23—"Nevertheless I am continually with Thee." "Nevertheless," in spite of the apparent deadness, in spite of the seeming dissipation of energy, in spite of the actual loss of power, the contact between his soul and the Spirit of the Eternal had never ceased. God had always been with him, even when he was unconscious of God; in the midst of death he had been in life. And the same idea appears in still stronger form in the words of verse

26—"My flesh and my heart faileth: but God is the strength of my heart, and my portion for ever." He sees in God not simply a Being who survives, but a Being who conserves. He might have contented himself with saying that though his own poor flesh and heart had failed, the life of the Eternal continued. But he says more than that; he declares that the life of the Eternal has become *his* life, the life of that very flesh and heart which had been subjected to death. God not only lives, but He lives in the psalmist's finite being, in his fainting heart, in his failing flesh. The one primal force not only abides, but keeps all other forces abiding. "I am continually with Thee:" we might have expected him to have said, "Thou art continually with *me*," yet the transposition is not accidental, and not void of significance. He wants to give emphasis to the fact that his own frail personality is made permanent by its union with the primal force; that his own fainting heart and failing flesh are rendered strong and enduring because they have come into contact with the life of the Eternal.

From this brief analysis, it will be seen what is implied by the seemingly irrelevant words, "Thou shalt guide me with Thy counsel, and afterward receive me to glory." At first sight one might be disposed to ask what this hope of immortality had to do with the matter; what was the connection of thought between the psalmist's recovery from his spiritual decline and his conviction that there existed a life of glory beyond? But when we look deeper, we see that the connection is close and intimate. What the psalmist really says is this: I have been already passing through a process of death. My spiritual life has been at the lowest ebb. I have been reduced very nearly to the condition of the beast of the field. Nevertheless, through the shadow of this valley, I have been preserved alive. I have been preserved by no strength of my own. That which has kept me alive is a continuous and unbroken contact which, unconsciously to myself, has subsisted between me and a higher life. In the valley of the shadow the life of the Eternal has been with me; God has held me by my right hand. Is not this the miniature of that greater transition still which I shall make in bodily death? If the life of the Eternal has been unconsciously guiding me in the sinking of my spiritual nature—if amid the seeming extinction of my moral being the cord that binds me to the Eternal has not been broken,—have I not every reason to believe that it will also remain unbroken in that hour when the powers of my physical being shall faint and fail?

It is in this light that a fact becomes intelligible which in any other light is inexplicable; we allude to the extreme hopefulness with which the writers of the Old Testament contemplate the eternity of

God. There is no subject from which the mind is naturally more apt to shrink; it overpowers the imagination, it overwhelms the reason. And yet no one can study the Old Testament records without being impressed with the truth that it is this, and nothing else than this, which constitutes the Jewish hope of futurity. We have often been struck with the direct statement of this fact in Habakkuk i. 12, "Art Thou not from everlasting, O Lord my God, mine Holy One? we shall not die." It will be seen that in those words the prophet actually bases his hope of immortality on his conviction of God's eternity. Natural instinct would have suggested the contrary; it would be disposed to read thus, "Art thou not from everlasting? what then are we, that we should expect to share Thine everlastingness?" The prophet's view on the other hand is, that because the attribute of eternity belongs to God, there is every reason to believe that it shall belong to man,—"*Thou* art from everlasting, therefore *we* shall not die." But if we read this utterance in the light of the seventy-third psalm, we shall find that the paradox vanishes, and that the conception of the prophet becomes luminously clear. If in the view of Judaism God had been simply a being outside the soul, it would have been presumption in the creature to have claimed eternity on the ground that He was eternal. But in the view of Judaism God was not a being outside the soul: He was the life of the soul itself. Every devout Jew felt what the writer of the seventy-third psalm felt when he declared that notwithstanding his sins and shortcomings he was continually with God. Eternity in his conception was not something to which his soul might attain after death; it was something to which his soul must attain *now*, if it would live for an hour. We find this thought expressed in the twenty-seventh verse of this psalm, "They that are far from Thee shall perish." The words are not meant as a prophetic statement, but as the statement of a universal principle. They do not tell what the psalmist conceives will happen in the future, but what he believes will always happen where the Spirit of the Eternal is absent from the life of man. To him God is the fountain of life, and absence from God is the fountain of death; to be near to God is to be within the range of immortalising influences, to be far from God is to perish. Accordingly, the Jew would have thoroughly understood these words of the New Testament, "Because I live, ye shall live also;" they are the exact parallel of the words of his own prophet, "Thou art from everlasting: we shall not die." God was everlasting, but God was a part of his own soul; his own soul, therefore, was a sharer in the divine eternity. Because he was able to say, "I am continually with Thee," he was equally able to add, "Thou art the strength of my heart, and my portion for ever."

It may seem, however, that in this exposition of the creed of Judaism we have already left science far behind. It may seem that we have risen into a region of transcendentalism whither the modern scientist would not seek to follow. What analogy, it may be asked, is there between the principle of conservation as it appears in the doctrine of evolution and the principle of conservation as it appears in the sentiment of the psalmist? In the doctrine of evolution the conserving principle is a law of nature; on the lips of the psalmist the conserving principle is a supernatural life. How can the scientist be asked to abandon his study of nature for the pursuit of that which is by hypothesis supernatural; to leave the investigation of known causes for the investigation of a cause which he himself holds to be conjectural? It was easy for the psalmist, believing as he did in an everlasting Personality, and believing that this everlasting Personality was in contact with his own soul, to look forward with confidence to the future and say, "Thou art the strength of my heart, and my portion for ever." But how can science entertain this confidence—that is to say, *scientifically* entertain it? The man of science may be also a man of faith, and as such he may look forward to the hope of the psalmist, but surely even then he will not maintain that his hope is scientific; must he not content himself at best with the modest ground that he is in possession of a faith which science has not yet disproved, and which he may be allowed to occupy till the light of reason shall come?

But are we quite sure that there is, after all, such a great gulf fixed between the Jewish conception of immortality and the scientific conception of conservation? May it not be found on a closer view that under different forms they are both essentially at one? What is the leading thought which underlies the idea of evolution? Is it not the refusal to admit any interruption in the chain of nature, the refusal to recognise any beginning of that chain? Evolution is the opposite of creation. It denies that there ever can have been in the universe a time when nothing existed, that there ever was a period in which there was an absolute blank of being. Accordingly, it holds that creation in an absolute sense is impossible. It declares that, go back so far as we may in the search for causes, we shall never go back so far as to find ourselves behind the birth of all causes; we shall always be in the presence of something from which other things have their being. Now this is commonly thought to be a statement allied to atheism. Yet if we consider it more deeply we shall see that, instead of being atheistic, it is precisely that statement which is made by every theist, and which every theist demands as the postulate of his creed. Theism as much as evolution is the denial of a possibility of blankness in the universe. The theist as strenuously as the evolutionist holds that there never was a time in which something was not. He too affirms that, however far we may go back in our search for causes, we will never arrive at that stage in which the principle of causation shall cease. Accordingly, he too is a powerful advocate for the doctrine that in an absolute sense creation is impossible. All the creations which the theist recognises are simply the creations made by a power already existing. He will not admit that power itself to be created; he declares it to be eternal. His very belief in God is an affirmation of the principle that there is in the universe a Being who is uncreated. Strange therefore as it may seem, the evolutionist and the creationist ultimately meet together. They both end in the same conclusion—the recognition that there is something eternal in the universe. They differ only as to the names by which they designate it; the evolutionist calls it Nature, the theist calls it God.

Now we are not going to dispute about the use of names, nor are we here concerned to inquire whether the scientific notion of Nature is compatible with the theistic notion of God. But we want to direct attention to a single point, and the only point which is here relevant. Whatever be the incongruity between the scientific notion of Nature and the theistic notion of God, there is one respect in which they are agreed; they both attribute to their object the possession of immortality. The God of the theist and the Nature of the scientist are both eternal; they are uncreated, and therefore they are immortal. It is impossible for the evolutionist to escape from this position without destroying the doctrine of evolution itself. If he decides to stop short in his search for causes, and to imagine a time in which the whole mechanism of the universe sprang into being spontaneously, he is of course at liberty to do so, but in doing so, he is deserting the field of evolution and taking possession of a field from which evolution is excluded. If he decides to remain in the sphere of evolution, he has thereby committed himself to the belief that there never was a time in which something was not —in other words, that the universe never had an absolute beginning. But in committing himself to this belief he is making to the religious sentiment a more important concession than he knows. He is really accepting all that the Jew accepted—the belief in the existence of a Power which has been of old for ever, which has existed before the mountains were brought forth, or the earth was formed, or the stars rolled in their courses. The evolutionist, just because he is an evolutionist, has signed a creed and confession wherein he recognises the fact that there is something immortal in the universe. It is not merely a recognition of the hope that something *will be* immortal; it is the admission that the existence of an immortal element has been already proved, the confession that Nature itself exhibits the presence of a power which has been able to subsist and to persist through all the changes incidental to material things.

We have said that this concession is more important than at first sight it might seem. It is not a scientific proof of the soul's immortality, but it helps to suggest a pathway whereby such a proof might become scientific. When we pass from the sphere of religion to the sphere of science, we are apt to be confronted by a spectre of despair. It seems to us at the outset as if there were no meeting-place between that life of the Eternal presupposed by Judaism and that life of nature recognised by science; the former is by definition immortal, the latter is to all outward appearance evanescent and transitory. One is disposed to ask what right the spirit of man has to imagine in the heart of the universe a permanence which the universe itself does not reveal. But the doctrine of evolution has helped us out of this difficulty. Inimical as it is supposed to be to the commonly received conclusions of the religious sentiment, it has yet supplied a missing link between the conclusions of that sentiment and the experiences of science. It has shown us that, however changeful and transitory the phenomena of the universe may be, there lies beneath these phenomena something which admits of neither change nor transition, something which abides continually amidst forms which are passing away, and preserves its distinctive character unaltered through all generations: it has revealed that the life of nature is already an immortal life.

Can we go any further in our analysis? Can we bring any nearer to ourselves this immortal element which science recognises in nature? We have seen, in speaking of Judaism, that the premiss, "Thou art from everlasting" does not of itself warrant the conclusion "we shall not die." To render that conclusion warranted, we must assume that the everlasting life of the Eternal has come into special contact with the human soul. Can we assume this in relation to that immortal element which science recognises in nature? Conceding that there exists in the universe an abiding Force, how does the immortality of that Force contribute to my immortality? Now there is a point admitted by science which is here well worthy of consideration. In the view of the evolutionist, in the view specially of Mr Herbert Spencer, the contact between the primal Force and the transitory forces of nature is not something to come: it is already an accomplished fact. The Force recognised by Mr Spencer is not merely a power that is persistent, but a power that is immanent. It not only exists unchanged through all the transmutations of natural phenomena; it exists unchanged in the heart of these transmutations. It is itself the source of these changes amongst which its permanence abides. It is present beneath all vicissitudes, it continues amid all fluctuations, it underlies all fleeting movements; it is the one amongst the many, the changeless amid the mutable. Here, therefore, as in the system of Judaism, we are confronted by a power which not only reveals immortality, but which reveals immortality in union with the things which are mortal. Without being liable to death, it lives amidst the dying; without being susceptible of either increase or diminution, it manifests its steadfastness through the increase and the diminution of the forces which it generates.

It may be said, however, that it is just here wherein the weakness of the argument consists. This abiding Force, existing unchanged through all manifestations, is yet unable to preserve these manifestations themselves from change. It underlies all phenomena, and its permanence is unaffected by all phenomena, but it *survives* all phenomena. It is independent of the life of the individual, and it dies not when the life of the individual dies, but it does not prevent the life of the individual from dying. The Force which abides under the water of a river is always the same Force; but not one drop of that water is for a moment the same: it exists in unity as a whole, but its unity is constituted by the perpetual disappearance and replacement of individual elements. The Force which underlies the light of the sun is for ever the same; yet not one beam of that light is for an instant identical: the ray on which we gaze this moment is not the ray on which we shall gaze the following moment; the unity lies only in our perception. These are not new facts: they are as old as the days of Heraclitus; but on that very account they have all the more claim to acceptance and all the more weight in argument. The argument which they offer would seem to be against an individual immortality. They lead us to ask what advantage there is in accepting the belief of the psalmist or in recognising the conclusion of the scientist. What does it matter whether there be or be not an abiding Force, if it abides only by the destruction of all individual forces? What does it signify whether we may or may not believe in the existence of a permanent principle in nature, if it is manifest to the most common observation that it is only the permanence of the river which remains amidst the disappearance of its individual drops? Is not the life of the individual the only thing which makes immortality desirable? Has either Judaism or modern science found a place for the being of the concrete form? Granting that there is a Power which exists from everlasting, and that this Power is not apart from, but immanent in the works of nature, is there not still wanted a link to that chain of reasoning which would connect the immortality of the everlasting Power with the immortality of those creatures which live and move within it?

Doubtless there is. It seems to us, however, that this link has been supplied by the testimony of the human soul. It is quite true that the river keeps its unity by the disappearance of its individual drops, that the light preserves its distinctiveness by the vanishing of its individual rays. The permanence of the abstract Force in every department of material nature exists only amid the death of the concrete and manifested forces. But there is one department of nature which some call material, and some immaterial, but to which, whatever view be taken of its character, the rule does not apply. Leaving out of account altogether every theory regarding the future, it is undeniably true that in the life of the present the individuality of the human soul is preserved alive amid the disappearance of other individualities. The abiding Force in nature which manifests itself by causing other concrete lives to die, manifests itself by causing this concrete life to live. There exists in the spirit of man a phenomenon which we call consciousness. What it is we do not know; whence it comes is a matter of dispute.

We shall not inquire into either of these questions; we shall not contend here either with the spiritualist or with the materialist; we shall keep to facts recognised by both. It is a fact recognised by both that, whatever be its essence and from whatever source it has come, consciousness now exists. It seems a very commonplace statement, and yet it contains one of the most striking of paradoxes. For what do we mean by that word consciousness? We mean nothing less than the continuity of individual existence in the midst of individual death. Everything around man is passing away. Every object on which he looks is disappearing from his view even as he gazes. That which he calls a river is not the river which he saw a moment ago; that which he terms the sunshine is a different sunshine from that which he designed to name. His own body is undergoing a perpetual series of changes; not one particle of the physical nature of the child remains in the physical nature of the man. And yet to the view of the man everything is identical—the river, the sunshine, the physical body. Nothing of his childhood remains in his manhood, yet his manhood feels that it is in essence the same as his childhood; he is quite convinced that he is the same individual who used to sport and play as a boy. This feeling is what we call consciousness. It is a unique fact in nature. It contradicts the experience of the river and the sunshine and every material thing. Here, for once in the universe, that absolute and primal Force which underlies all phenomena and subsists through the death of phenomena, has manifested itself by keeping a phenomenon alive. Here, for the first time in the circle of creation, we are confronted by the spectacle of a concrete force which has been able to subsist through the changes of other forces, and has held its individual life undiminished amid the complete dissolution of its whole environment. Consciousness, as we know it, is like a mariner who is perpetually shipwrecked but never drowned. Everything around it is submerged; masts, sails, and rigging are rent asunder; the planks of the ship itself are severed by the waves. But through the surrounding destruction consciousness remains intact; it stands unharmed upon the sea of life, and claims its continuity amid the perishable.

Let us now apply this truth of experience to the words of the psalmist of Israel,—" My flesh and my heart faileth: but God is the strength of my heart, and my portion for ever." He had, as we have seen, been passing through a spiritual crisis—his old self had passed away, his old ideals had been submerged, his old hopes had perished. Yet, amidst a total change of environment, amidst the failing of the flesh and the fainting of the heart, he was conscious that the essence of his personality remained the same. He was conscious that his individual nature, at the very time when naturally it ought to have died, had been preserved alive by the power of the Eternal. He concluded that if the power of the Eternal was able to preserve his individual life through a complete change of environment in this world, it was equally able to preserve his individual life through that complete change of environment which should mark his transition from this world into the world to come; and he expressed his confidence in that conclusion by uttering the words of hope and consolation,—" Thou shalt guide me with Thy counsel, and afterward receive me to glory." The psalmist believed in a principle of conservation which was able at the end of life to usher him into another life; and he did so precisely on the ground that he had discovered a principle of conservation which even in the present life had been the sole source of his continuance. Far removed as his conception seems to be from the scientific standpoint of the nineteenth century, we have found that essentially the standpoints are the same. We have found that the evolutionist of our age, like the psalmist of ancient Israel, recognises in the universe a principle of conservation —recognises the existence not only of something which is itself immortal, but of something which has the power to immortalise. We have seen that this principle of immortality, though throughout material things it manifests itself amid the death of concrete forms, has yet in the consciousness of the human soul exerted an immortalising power. Of every particle of man's physical organisation it may be said, "My flesh and my heart faileth." The house of his earthly tabernacle has, even while he dwells on earth, again and again been dissolved, again and again constructed anew. Often has it been sown in corruption and raised in incorruption, sown in weakness and raised in power, sown in dishonour and raised in glory, sown a natural body and raised a spiritual body. Yet through all these changes the consciousness has persisted, through all these burials and resurrections the personality has remained the same. The individual man has lived amid the destruction of his first environment; the tenant has retained possession of the field after the house which was built on it has been dissolved. All this by the verdict of modern science has been effected through the agency of that primal and absolute Force which underlies all things and comprehends all things. With such premisses as these to rest upon, is not the modern scientist entitled to draw the conclusion which was drawn by the ancient psalmist—that the nature of the universe warrants a hope of immortality? Is he, too, not entitled to say that a Power which is able to preserve him from death in the midst of earthly life is able to preserve him from death when earthly life has come to its close? If the abiding Force of nature has kept him alive already through the many dissolutions of his earthly tabernacle, has he not reason to hope that it will keep him alive in that final dissolution wherein his latest earthly tabernacle shall pass away? If he can now say, amid the present failing of the flesh, "Thou art the strength of my heart," may he not expect to say in the latest failing of all, "Thou shalt afterward receive me to glory"?

CHAPTER XIII.

CONCLUSION.

We have now passed under review the leading doctrines of the religious sentiment. We have placed them side by side with the doctrines of modern science, in order to subject them to the full glare of comparison. As the result of that comparison we have arrived at a definite conclusion. In every single case we have been led to the inference that the light of modern science has not thrown into the shade the ancient verdict of the religious sentiment. We have found that the faith of the Book of Psalms is not an anachronism; that notwithstanding the vast interval which divides it from modern culture, it is still capable of being made a manual of devotion to the scientific mind.

The question on which we have been engaged is a vital one, more vital than any other question of apologetics. All other questions of apologetics relate to the circumference of religion; this refers to its centre. It has frequently been asked whether the scepticism of the nineteenth century is more or less virulent than the scepticism of the preceding age. We are disposed to say that in one sense it is less virulent, in another sense, more. The scepticism of the previous century was louder than that of our own. It was more vehement, more ribald, more polemical; it attacked religion for the sake of attack, and with the desire of obtaining the victory. The scepticism of the nineteenth century is never ribald, and rarely abusive; its attack is not generally prompted by the desire of victory, but oftener by a sad compulsion. The modern man of science, when he assails the truths of the past, assails them frequently against his will. However strongly he may protest that they are at variance with the modern conception of nature, he is not ashamed in his inmost heart to acknowledge that he rejects them with sorrow, and parts from them with regret. To this extent the scepticism of the nineteenth century is more mellowed than the scepticism of the eighteenth. But from another point of view it is stronger. Its mode of attack is softer, but its point of attack is more central. The scepticism of the eighteenth century was only an assault upon outworks; the scepticism of the nineteenth has laid siege to the citadel. The attack on the outworks might be conducted, and was conducted, by men who professed to have the spirit of religion, and who, had the outworks been destroyed, would have professed to retain the spirit of religion still. But the attack which is made by the scepticism of our age is one which, if successful, must destroy the spirit of religion itself. The question is no longer whether a particular book of the Bible is genuine. It is no longer whether miracles are possible. It is no longer even whether supernatural Christianity can be recognised as true. It is whether there be or be not a supernatural at all. It is whether the conception of God is any longer compatible with that conception of nature at which the scientist has now arrived. In the controversy of the former age men might lose one outwork without abandoning their system of defence; they might even erect another bulwark in the place where the last had been destroyed. But the scepticism of our age, if successful, must render the future defence of religion impossible — for it is concerned mainly with the question whether religion has a right to exist.

But there is another respect in which the scepticism of the nineteenth century is concerned with a vital question. The discussion which it raises must be settled by each mind now and here. The subject will not bear a suspension of judgment. The theological controversies of the past were of a different order. Men might weigh the arguments for and against any doctrine, and might then decide to take the case *ad avizandum*. They might refuse, and refuse with advantage, to make up their minds on a question which had strong arguments on both sides, and on whose decision important issues depended. This was probably the attitude actually assumed by the large majority of those who witnessed the theological discussions of the last century. They contemplated the battle between the Christian and the Deist, between the Trinitarian and the Arian, with the interest of spectators rather than of partisans. They were more interested in the winning of the argument than in the establishment of the truth; they eulogised the victor, and then they hung up the question. But the question of the nineteenth century cannot be hung up. It relates not to a dogma but to a sentiment—the religious sentiment itself. It is concerned with the inquiry whether the heart's conception of God is compatible with the intellect's conception of Nature. Suppose that a man should decide to suspend his judgment on that subject. Suppose that to accomplish this end he should resolve to keep his religious sentiment for the present in abeyance, what would be the result of such a course? If prolonged indefinitely, it could only end in the destruction of the religious sentiment. An intellectual dogma can be recalled at any time. The mind may refuse to think of it for a succession of years, and at the end of that period may come back to it with renewed freshness and vigour. But to suspend for a series of years an exercise of the religious sentiment is inevitably to destroy that sentiment. The religious sentiment, like every other sense, can only continue to subsist by continuing to be exercised. If it cease to be exercised for an indefinite period, it will die. Accordingly, the question at issue between the religion and the science of our age admits of no postponement. The mind of each individual man must settle it for himself, and settle it previous to entering on any other theological field. It is only through the presence and the power of the religious sentiment that any theological field can be trodden, and to suspend this presence and this power is effectually to bar the gate against all further progress.

It is from a forecast of the extreme gravity and importance of this question that we have been prompted to devote to it the preceding pages. We have tried to express on paper a record of that inward struggle which we ourselves have felt, and a record of that process by which, in our own mind, the struggle has been lulled to rest. It by no means follows, of course, that the train of thought delineated in these pages will have a similar effect upon the reader; the amount of evidence which to one mind would be absolutely satisfactory may to another be trifling and insufficient. If, however, we have in any measure succeeded in directing attention to a possible harmony between the conclusions of the scientific intellect and the intuitions of the religious sentiment, we shall have done all that it was in our purpose to do. The gain, indeed, to religion from success in such an effort would be greater than at first sight one might naturally suppose. It is not that any new light would be thrown on any special theological system. It is not that a solution would be offered of problems which tend to present themselves as contradictions. The advantage gained would be of a more preliminary nature. The solution of the question which we have proposed to answer would derive its main value from this; that it would clear the way for asking other questions. The danger of that difficulty which presses on the nineteenth century lies in the fact that, until it is removed, it bars the threshold of all inquiry. If it be a matter of doubt whether the religious sentiment is still entitled to retain its validity, there must, in the meantime, be a paralysis of all religious thought; and a paralysis existing in the meantime is in danger of becoming a perpetual one. As a preliminary to all investigation, as a condition necessary to all inquiry, it is requisite that first and foremost there should be an annulling of that seeming divorce which exists between the conclusions of science and the verdict of religious intuition; it is only in the annulling of that divorce that religious thought can regain that energy and elasticity which are demanded for the prosecution of study.

But let us consider, on the other hand, what would

be the effect of a marriage between the doctrines of the scientist and the intuitions of the psalmist. It would be something more than a compromise. It would not merely indicate that henceforth science and religion would be allowed to pursue their separate ways unmolested by one another. It would not even merely indicate that difficulties in religion might henceforth be solved on the principle of Bishop Butler, by producing equal difficulties in the sphere of science. Whatever might be the advantage of such a power, it would amount to less than the advantage of a marriage; it would, at best, be simply an alliance. What a marriage between science and religion contemplates, is a result much deeper than that; it is nothing less than a transference into the one of the thought peculiar to the other. It contemplates the power to look with a religious eye on that system of nature comprehended by modern science; it contemplates the ability to look with a scientific eye on that world of religion comprehended by the ancient psalmist. When the union to which we look forward be complete, it shall involve an exchange of predicates; it shall give a religious view of nature and a scientific view of Providence. It shall enable a man in the field of physical science to feel that he is engaged in an exercise of devotion; it shall enable a man in the field of actual devotion to feel that he is pursuing a track in harmony with physical science.

This, and nothing less than this, is the degree of unanimity which is necessary to form an adequate union between the speculations of the nineteenth century and the meditations of ancient Israel. It is not enough that science and religion should cease to fight against each other; it is not even enough that they should consent to help each other. Their relation will not be perfect as long as their two fields lie contiguous; it will not be perfect as long as there are two fields at all. To consummate their union the two fields must become one. When I take up the book of the psalmist and read the words, "O Lord, Thou hast searched me, and known me; Thou knowest my down-sitting and mine uprising, Thou understandest my thought afar off," I must be able to feel that I am speaking to that primal Force which presides over the law of evolution. When I take up the writings of Mr Herbert Spencer and read how that primal Force which presides over the law of evolution manifests itself in all things, I must be able to feel that I am listening to a description of that very mode of divine immanence which the psalmist eulogises as the Searcher and Knower of my heart.

We have now to observe that if this union should ever be completed, it will complete the triumph of the Bible as an appeal to human need. There are two things which this nineteenth century requires as the conditions of a developed religion—a perfect ideal of man, and a scientific doctrine of God. It is conceded by all classes that the former has been already realised. In the moral ideal of the Son of Man the New Testament has taken its place as one of the most powerful forces of social life. The science of our day, however much it may be opposed to Christian dogmatics, has reverently bowed its head before the ideal of Christian purity. It is on this ground that the New Testament is, in our age, generally preferred to the Old. Science freely admits that it has not outgrown Christian morality; it only professes to have outgrown Jewish monotheism. If, however, it should be found that Jewish monotheism is no more an anachronism than Christian morality, we shall at last have in the Bible a complete manual of devotion. We have confessedly received an ideal of purity which is fully abreast of the age—an ideal which has not been superannuated by the advance of time or the development of culture, but which stands in the blaze of the modern light, with its eye undimmed, and its natural strength unabated. It would complete the picture if the satisfaction of man's moral ideal could be supplemented by the satisfaction of his intellectual one, if the Old Testament portrait of God should be found to be as capable of modern contemplation as the New Testament portrait of man.

There is a point in connection with this subject

which is well worthy of attention. Between the morality of the New Testament and the religious faith of the Old there exists one great analogy. If we inquire what is the reason of that marvellous ascendancy which the morality of the Gospel has acquired over all other moralities, we shall find that, humanly speaking, it lies in the fact of its many-sidedness. The moral system of the Gospel does not profess to come with original elements; it professes to derive its originality from the fact that it combines old elements. It is essentially a system of reconciliation. It gathers together those ethical creeds of the past which in their isolation had stood to one another in relations of mutual enmity. It unites under one rule systems which when standing apart had seemed incapable of any other attitude than hostility. It combines the philosophy of the Epicurean, the philosophy of the Stoic, and the philosophy of the Platonist. It incorporates the tendency to self-preservation with two other tendencies, which in the light of ordinary nature are supposed to be its opposites—the love of our neighbour, and the love of God. It leaves out of account no phase of the human mind, it eliminates from its view no element of human nature. The distinctive feature of its provision is its universal adaptiveness, its power to meet man in every possible sphere and in every possible circumstance. Hence it is that the Gospel morality has been universally accepted as an ideal of that life which man ought to live. It has been received by the representatives of every country, and kindred, and people, and tongue—has been eulogised by the voices of a multitude which no man can number. The catholicity of the praise has proceeded from the catholicity of the system. Men have yielded their homage to that which has manifested an interest in their practical needs, and in proportion as their needs have been various, the homage has been correspondingly various. The Gospel morality can claim to be an original power, because for the first time in history it has succeeded in finding a meeting-place for the ethical systems of the past.

But if we consider the religious faith of the Old Testament, we shall find that it bears precisely the same relation to other faiths as the morality of the New Testament does to other moralities. The Old Testament conception of God is a monotheistic conception; but it is not merely on account of its monotheism that it has been able to survive so long. It is rather because it embodies a system of monotheism so rich and varied as to comprehend within its folds other and contrary systems. The Supreme Being of Judaism is commonly thought to possess exclusively the attribute of unity; this is a mistake. He is indeed presented to our view as one God, besides whom there is no other; but within this unity of nature He encloses a vast variety. On the very opening page of the Jewish Scriptures the divine image is declared not to be single but dual; and to be made in the image of God is said to be equivalent to being created male and female. In this bold utterance Judaism has already united elements which in other religions have remained either hostile or separate. It has recognised in the unity of the divine nature the operation of a twofold life, the action of a force which is masculine and the receptivity of a force which is feminine. And all through the Jewish history we find ourselves practically reminded of this dual life of God. Sometimes we are called to contemplate the energy of a masculine Divine Will, ruling arbitrarily in the armies of heaven and speaking imperatively among the inhabitants of the earth; at such times the spirit of the worshipper cannot feel the sense of freedom. At other times, again, we are confronted by an exactly opposite spectacle. We find ourselves in the presence of a Being whose prerogative it is to listen to the supplications of His creatures, to hear the groaning of the prisoner, to loose those that are appointed to death; the masculine has given place to the feminine element, and the soul of the worshipper rises into the liberty of the sons of God.

If we look at the subject from another point of view, we shall meet with a new illustration of the same dualism. In one aspect the God of the Old

Testament is intimately connected with His works. He is the breath of that life in which all things live, and move, and have their being. No pantheist could more strongly express his sense of the union subsisting between the world and God than do the writers of the Jewish Scriptures at certain moments of their religious experience. Take, for example, that wondrous hymn of praise to the God of nature which appears in the twenty-ninth psalm. Every object in the universe, however minute, every act in the universe, however trifling, is equally declared to be a note in the voice of God. The voice of the Lord is pronounced to be the moving cause of all things. It resounds in the waters, it rolls in the thunder, it breaks the cedars, it divides the flames of fire, it shakes the wilderness, it presides over the birth of creature forms. Nay, its influence does not stop here. The same voice which resounds in the waters and rolls in the thunder is declared to be the moving power of those comparatively humble forces which emanate from human hearts. When the psalmist says, "In His temple doth every one speak of His glory," he designs to convey the thought that the hymns of praise which issue from earnest souls are themselves simply the utterance of the divine voice within; and that the religious life of man, instead of being a mere groping of the human spirit after God, is in reality the Spirit of God Himself directing our spirits into communion with His life.

All this indicates the sense of a very intimate union between the human and the divine, a union infinitely nearer than that of any earthly relationship, a union equal to that which any pantheist could desire. But it is not long before we are impressed with the fact that in the mind of the Jewish writers there was another side of the subject. There were times in their religious experience in which the object of their worship presented Himself in an opposite light. There were times in which their sense of God's greatness manifested itself not in the contemplation of His infinite nearness but in the thought of His infinite distance. If at one moment the psalmist of Israel is impressed with the proximity of the divine voice to the voices of nature, at another he is overwhelmed with a conviction of the boundless gulf which separates the life of the creature from the life of the Creator; at such seasons he is disposed to cry, "What is man, that Thou art mindful of him?" If in the one aspect he touches a side of God's nature which is allied to pantheism, in another he gets a glimpse of that side which is allied to deism; if in the one he feels the sympathy of the mystic, he experiences in the other the distance of the agnostic. It is by reason of this double consciousness of God that the writers of the Old Testament seem divided between ascribing to Him the attributes of personality and the mystery of a Power that transcends description. Sometimes they speak of Him in terms purely anthropomorphic; they describe Him as smelling a sweet savour, as looking down from heaven upon the children of men, as coming down from the skies to examine the Tower of Babel. At others, and these are the majority, they insist pertinaciously on the impossibility of representing God. They declare that He is beyond the power of definition, and that it is impious to define Him. It is this which has prompted the second commandment of the Decalogue, "Thou shalt not make unto thee any graven image." It is this which has inspired the later Isaiah to exclaim, "To whom then will ye liken God? or what likeness will ye compare unto Him?" He feels that to stand beneath the canopy of heaven ought alone to be enough to refute the tendency to image-representation. The boundlessness and fathomlessness of the abysses of nature reveal to the eye of the prophet the presence of a Power which is indeed all-comprehending, but which at the same time is uncomprehended, and it seems to him that it would be blasphemy towards that Power if man should seek to represent what the heaven of heavens cannot contain. "Why askest thou after my name?" are the words put into the divine lips in the narrative of that marvellous struggle which the spirit of Jacob experienced under the stars of Peniel. It shows that already in that early age the spirit of Judaism had declared itself, and had declared itself in favour of worshipping an invisible God. It had refused to admit that any name would represent the Almighty, that any definition would describe the directive power of nature. It had elected to place its faith in a Being whom the eye was unable to see, had consented to repose its confidence in a Power which the intellect could not understand.

The truth is, notwithstanding the charge of narrowness which is so frequently preferred against the Jewish worship, the religious intellect of the nation is distinguished by its catholicity. The God of the Old Testament is presented to us in an attitude which makes Him potentially the God of the whole earth, which already predicts the time when He shall be known and acknowledged amongst all nations. The ancient Israelite approached the object of his worship under a variety of names, and he employed the variety just in order to indicate that none of the names was final, none adequate to represent the whole. When he wanted to speak of Him as He manifested Himself in nature, he called Him Elohim. When he desired to describe Him as He revealed Himself in the national history, he termed Him Jehovah. When he sought to portray Him as the object of religious adoration and the source of religious aspiration, he addressed Him by the name of Adonai. The variety of appellatives indicated a variety of aspects. It implied that the God of the Old Testament was not to be pictured in a single form, not to be revealed in a solitary attribute. He was to present a different phase of His being to the different moods of separate minds—nay, to the different moods which distinguished the same mind at separate times. It was through this variety of aspect that the God of the Old Testament remained an object of worship to a nation which many times changed its nationality. Of all the peoples of the earth, the children of Israel have had the most diverse fortunes. Again and again they have been transplanted from their native soil. From the days when the patriarch Abraham migrated into Egypt, until the days when the Macedonian empire stretched its arms over the Jewish nation, they have never retained a permanent possession of their soil. In every one of these transplantings their national consciousness was modified; in every one of these foreign sojourns their national life was affected. And yet it is a crowning testimony to the universality of their religion that in the midst of all these changes their worship remained unchanged. It is a crowning testimony to the essential catholicity of Judaism, that even in so foreign a soil as that of ancient Alexandria it was able under the inspiration of a Philo Judæus to take root in a philosophic form. Such constancy amid surrounding mutability could only have manifested itself in a faith which was naturally catholic in its sympathies and essentially cosmopolitan in its aims.

It would not, therefore, surprise us to find that

the faith of the Jewish Scriptures has been able to stand yet one other transplanting. It would not surprise us to discover that a religious sentiment which has been capable of subsisting through so many different modes of culture has been capable of subsisting through yet one mode more. It would not be strange if a worship which could adapt itself to so diverse a mould as the philosophy of Alexandria should succeed in adapting itself to the scientific culture of the nineteenth century. That it has so succeeded, it has been the aim of these pages to prove. If the proof has been satisfactory, if the religious sentiment of the Old Testament is really recognised to be in harmony with the scientific spirit of this age, we may obtain light on a practical problem which has often appeared dark and difficult. There are two forces at work in modern society for the propagation of missionary enterprise—the force of scientific education and the force of religious culture. It is popularly thought that these have a totally separate province; it is not seldom feared that they may lead to opposite issues. The religious missionary may teach the truths of religion; but if the scientific missionary should teach at the same time the truths of evolution, will not the seed be rooted up in the very hour of planting? The question is a pertinent and a perplexing one, and one which presses for an early answer. Surely there could be no answer more well-timed and more satisfactory than to show that the provinces of the two forces are not separate after all; that the missionary interest of religion is the same as the missionary interest of science; and that the study of the laws of Nature will prove identical with the study of the law of God.

PRINTED BY WILLIAM BLACKWOOD AND SONS.

www.ingramcontent.com/pod-product-compliance
Lightning Source LLC
Chambersburg PA
CBHW021152230426
43667CB00006B/364